PICTURE ENCYCLOPEDIA

— OF —

PASSENGER
SHIPS
1955

PICTURE ENCYCLOPEDIA

OF

PASSENGER SHIPS

1955

WILLIAM H. MILLER

FONTHILL

Cover: The Italian liner *Cristoforo Colombo* (1954).

First published in Great Britain in 2026 by
Fonthill
An imprint of
Pen & Sword Books Ltd
Yorkshire – Philadelphia
www.fonthill.media

Copyright © William H. Miller, 2026

ISBN 978-1-03615-647-3

The right of William H. Miller to be identified as
Author of this work has been asserted by him in accordance
with the Copyright, Designs and Patents Act 1988.

A CIP catalogue record for this book
is available from the British Library.

Typeset in SabonLTStd 11.5/15 by
SJmagic DESIGN SERVICES, India.
Printed and bound in the UK by CPI Group (UK) Ltd, Croydon, CR0 4YY

The Publisher's authorised representative in the EU for product
safety is Authorised Rep Compliance Ltd., Ground Floor,
71 Lower Baggot Street, Dublin D02 P593, Ireland.
www.arccompliance.com

For a complete list of Pen & Sword titles please contact
PEN & SWORD BOOKS LIMITED
George House, Units 12 & 13, Beevor Street, Off Pontefract Road,
Barnsley, South Yorkshire, S71 1HN, England
E-mail: enquiries@pen-and-sword.co.uk
Website: www.pen-and-sword.co.uk

or

PEN AND SWORD BOOKS
1950 Lawrence Rd, Havertown, PA 19083, USA
E-mail: uspen-and-sword@casematepublishers.com
Website: www.penandswordbooks.com

Foreword

As a child beginning in the 1950s, our family moved overseas three times—and always by ship. These were adventures for my parents and for my brother and myself. In doing so, I became interested in travel, especially travel by ship. In those days, you could travel just about anywhere on a ship.

My father worked for a big, international company. His first overseas assignment was to India. It was 1955 and we began with a crossing from New York to Genoa, Italy, on board the *Cristoforo Colombo*. We traveled comfortably in cabin class and I especially remember the swimming pool and sun deck. In Italy, we later joined another Italian ship, the *Asia*, which took us through the Suez Canal and delivered us to Bombay, where we lived for almost two years. When we finally returned to the States, my father first wanted to visit London and so we sailed from Bombay to England on a big P&O liner, the *Orcades*. Later, we headed home, from Southampton to New York, on board the *Queen Elizabeth*. The *Queen Elizabeth* was the world's largest liner, and it certainly seemed so to my young mind. It was huge!

The second overseas assignment was to Sao Paulo. We sailed from New York to Rio de Janeiro on the *Brazil*—and then returned after another two years but to New Orleans on a smaller passenger-cargo ship, the *Del Norte*.

Finally, the third relocation was to Japan and Hong Kong. We set sail from San Francisco to Yokohama on the *President Wilson* and then, with another two years past, we headed home from Hong Kong on another big P&O liner, the *Iberia*.

Bill Miller has reminded me in this book of the many and varied passenger ships and of their diverse routings. What a wealth of ships! It is absolute maritime nostalgia! Now some seventy years since my first voyage, I am happy to be a part of this compilation.

Three long blasts on the whistles, streamers being tossed and so off we go!

Victor Young
Honolulu, Hawaii
Summer 2025

Lloyd Triestino's *Victoria* makes a special stop during a summer cruise at Rhodes. (*Author's Collection*)

Acknowledgements

Creating a book is like manning a ship—it takes many hands. As the author, I might be the equal to the chief purser. I develop a title, gather materials and then create. With that, many thanks to Fonthill Media, to Alan Sutton, Jay Slater, Josh Greenland and staff, for taking on this project.

And added first class thanks to Michael Hadgis, Anthony La Forgia and Tim Noble. Added special thanks to Barry J. Eagles, the late Mick Lindsay, Captain James McNamara and Captain Justin Zizes.

Other individuals that assisted include the late Frank Andrews, the late Frank Braynard, Philippe Brebant, J. K. Byass, the Cronican-Arroyo Collection, the late Alex Duncan, the late John Gillespie, Andy Hernandez, David Hutchings, the late Norman Knebel, the late Vincent Messina, Peter Plowman, the late S. W. Rawlings, the late Willie Tinnemeyer and David Williams.

Companies and organizations that have assisted include American Export Lines, American President Lines, British India Steam Navigation Co Ltd, Companhia Colonial, Cunard Line, Flying Camera Inc, Greek Line, Holland-Africa Line, Holland-America Line, Messageries Maritimes, Moran Towing & Transportation Co, Norwegian America Line, P&O Cruises, Port Authority of New York & New Jersey, Royal Mail Lines, Steamship Historical Society of America, Swedish American Line, Union-Castle Line and the World Ship Society, especially the Port of New York Branch.

Otherwise, any and all omissions are sincerely regretted.

Contents

The *Independence* makes a late afternoon call at Algeciras. (*Cronican-Arroyo Collection*)

Introduction

As a boy, beginning in the 1950s, my family supported and greatly encouraged my budding interest in passenger ships. My mother bought me toy boats, my father took me across the Hudson from our home in Hoboken to see the great liners in closer range, and my grandfather (a retired policeman) took me aboard liners on sailing day, and then sometimes on quiet afternoons while waiting in port. He also took me on ferryboat rides, the Lackawanna Railway ferry out of Hoboken and, on longer trips, aboard the famed Staten Island ferry. It would be my mini "ocean voyage". And then there was Aunt Lillian, who actually worked in the shipping district, in fact in the grand Cunard Building at 25 Broadway in Lower Manhattan, but for the marine division of the New York Central Railroad. She was my steady supply of countless shipping magazines, which I would read and re-read— and sometimes cut-up and then use the clippings and photos for my scrapbooks. Among these copies was the *Official Steamship Guide*. It was a monthly compendium of steamship lines, some serving in the most remote areas of the globe, with office addresses, rates, routes and sometimes the latest sailing schedules. Occasionally, say on a rainy afternoon, I would sit and plot imaginary voyages—to South America, to Australia, even around-the-world—and usually on a variety of interconnecting passenger liners. I might plot a crossing from New York to Southampton, then a long voyage out to Sydney, then back to Europe and finally home to New York.

At least two of my teachers were very keen travelers on liners. Miss Marnell set off in late June and usually on a voyage that lasted the two months of the summer holidays. One year, as I remember, it was forty-five days on the *Caronia* to the North Cape and Scandinavia. Another year, it was fifty days around the Pacific onboard the *Orsova*. Still another, she was off to South America for six weeks on a Grace Line passenger-cargo ship that carried fifty passengers. Meanwhile, Mr Pescatore had a Belgian wife and so that meant each and every summer to Europe and always by ship. Often, it was aboard a ship of the Holland-America Line, but sometimes it was a fast passage on the *United States* or the *Queen Elizabeth*. The family also had relatives in north Africa and this meant mid-summer journeys by train down to Marseilles and then crossings on smaller French passenger ships. It was all very exciting—and ignited something in me to one day travel by ship and wander about on the seven seas.

My idea for this book (and possibly two more volumes, in 1965 and for 1975) is not only to share photos of almost 200 ships, but as a glimpse, a reminder, of the vast and very diverse passenger ship services of the mid-fifties. I had to limit the ships to those of 10,000 tons and larger. Listing smaller ships, those "little steamers," might have required a second book. And remember, of course, that in 1955, the airlines and their speedy aircraft had yet to offer serious competition. Travelers still much preferred the traditional sea routes.

1955 was in fact selected because it was ten years after the end of World War II, so lots of new tonnage joined older, pre-war ships in worldwide operations. It was also three years before airlines captured the majority of passengers on the illustrious North Atlantic and over a decade before jet services overtook routes east of Suez. Between decades, say by 1965 and then 1975, the face of passenger travel by sea changed and the great cast of ships did as well.

So with imagination sparked and with luggage in hand—and perhaps a trunk or two—we can head off to the likes of New York, Southampton, Lisbon, Genoa, Cape Town, Hong Kong, Sydney or San Francisco and catch a ship and begin a journey that might create magical memories.

And hopefully, I have created another journey—a trip along maritime memory lane.

Bill Miller
Secaucus, New Jersey
Winter 2025

The Ships

Accra & Apapa

Constructed in the late 1940s for Britain's Elder Dempster Lines and for the West African colonial trade, this pair of 11,500-ton sister ships carried 259 first class passengers and a small, aft deck third class for twenty-four. The ships sailed in rotation with the larger *Aureol* between Liverpool, Freetown, Takoradi, Lagos, Bathurst and Apapa. First class included a suite with sitting room and most other cabins had private bathroom facilities.

The handsome *Apapa* at Liverpool. (*Barry J. Eagles Collection*)

AFRICA & EUROPA

This smart-looking pair were very popular on the East & South African run—sailing from Trieste, Venice and Brindisi to Port Said, the Suez Canal, Aden, Mogadishu, Mombasa, Dar es Salaam, Beira, Durban, Cape Town, Port Elizabeth and East London. Sailings were made at 3–4 week intervals. Designed for 148 first class and 298 tourist class passengers, the 11,500-ton sisterships were notably fully air-conditioned. All first class cabins had private bathrooms; tourist class rooms had mostly semi-private facilities.

The smart-looking *Africa*. (*Norman Knebel Collection*)

AKAROA

This veteran 15,300-ton ship, owned by Britain's Shaw Savill Line, dated from 1914. Carrying only 182 passengers in one class, it was used in New Zealand service—from London via Panama to Auckland and Wellington.

The veteran *Akaroa* seen at Capetown. (*Author's Collection*)

ALBERTO DODERO & YAPEYU

This modern-looking pair, at 11,500 tons, were Dutch-built for Dodero Line's low-fare/migrant service between Hamburg, Amsterdam, Vigo, Rio de Janeiro, Santos, Montevideo and Buenos Aires. Each ship was fitted for some 800 passengers—with a small, top-deck first class (for thirteen passengers). Tourist quarters were in large cabins and dormitories.

The *Alberto Dodero* and its sister were long and low. (*Norman Knebel Collection*)

ALBERTVILLE, BAUDOUINVILLE, CHARLESVILLE, ELISABETHVILLE & LEOPOLDVILLE

This colonial service operated from Antwerp via Tenerife to the Belgian Congo, Lobito and Matadi. The voyage between Antwerp and Lobito took fourteen days. There were weekly sailings from Antwerp. The ships offered comfortable quarters for 205–250 passengers and amenities included an outdoor pool, a gift shop, hair salon and children's nursery.

The *Albertville* at sea. (*Willie Tinnemeyer Collection*)

ALCANTARA

This grand old liner, dating from 1926, had been a twin-stacker but was rebuilt in 1935 with a single stack. After World War II it resumed South American service on the East Coast of South America run from Southampton. Teamed with the slightly larger and newer *Andes* (qv), passenger accommodation on the 22,607-ton *Alcantara* was arranged for 220 in first class, 180 second class, and 460 third class.

Above: The stately *Alcantara* seen at Cherbourg.
(*Author's Collection*)

Left: An artistic brochure cover for the *Alcantara*.
(*Author's Collection*)

AMERICA

Completed in 1940 and all but immediately pressed into wartime service as a 9,000 capacity troopship (also being renamed *USS West Point)*, this 33,961-ton liner had her debut on its intended North Atlantic service (between New York, Cobh, Le Havre, Southampton and Bremerhaven) in 1946. Carrying 1,046 passengers, this ship was a trans-ocean favorite and running mate to the far larger and faster *United States* (qv).

New York's Luxury Liner Row in June 1960—the *Media* (top), *Caronia, Queen Mary, Britannic, Liberte, America, Saturnia* and *Independence*. (*Port Authority of New York & New Jersey*)

ANDES

A division of Furness, Withy & Co, this London-based firm had a long history serving South America. Two big liners, the 26,900-ton *Andes* and the 22,500-ton *Alcantara*, maintained the luxury service. Southampton via Cherbourg, Vigo, Lisbon and Las Palmas to Rio de Janeiro, Santos, Montevideo and Buenos Aires. The run from Southampton to Buenos Aires took twenty-one days. Each carried passengers in two classes.

Above: The luxurious *Andes* arriving at Cherbourg with *the Queen Mary* behind. (*Royal Mail Lines*)

Left: A poster promoting the *Andes*. (*Norman Knebel Collection*)

ANDREA DORIA & CRISTOFORO COLOMBO

As Italy's finest post-war liners, the pair, completed in 1952 and 1954, were dubbed "Renaissance ships". Used on the Naples–Genoa–Cannes–Gibraltar–New York service carrying 1,250 passengers in three classes, they were especially splendid ships; fully air-conditioned, five swimming pools, modern décor.

Above: In a view at New York dated September 1956, the *United States* (top), *America* and *Cristoforo Colombo* are seen together in port. (*Port Authority of New York & New Jersey*)

Below: An Italian passage ticket. (*Author's Collection*)

ANGOLA & MOCAMBIQUE

British-built, these 12,900-ton sisterships were the largest and finest yet for Portugal's Compania Nacional de Navegacao and their Lisbon–West, South & East African service. Carrying approximately 720 passengers in first, second, third and fourth classes (the latter for migrants, troops, colonial police, etc). Round voyages—between Lisbon, Funchal, Sao Tome, Luanda, Lobito, Mossamedes, Cape Town, Lourenco Marques, Beira, Mozambique and Nacala—took forty-five days. The previous schedule took a month longer.

The *Angola* seen at Capetown. (*Norman Knebel Collection*)

ANNA C

Built in 1929 as the *Southern Prince* for the British-flag Prince Line, it was sold after wartime trooping duties to the Costa Line, Linea "C". The 11,736 tonner was remodeled (for 500 first, second and third class passengers) and entered service in March 1948 as the *Anna C*. The general routing was from Genoa, Naples, Cannes and Lisbon to Funchal, Rio de Janeiro, Santos, Montevideo and Buenos Aires.

Arrival for the *Anna C*.
(*Author's Collection*)

ANNA SALEN

Built in 1940 as an American freighter, but soon rebuilt as an escort aircraft carrier. Rebuilt in the late 1940s as a 1,700 capacity migrant ship for Sweden's Salen Line, the 492-foot-long ship was used on varied sailings: North Atlantic, South Atlantic and to Australia. The majority of the ship's passengers were carried in six- and eight-berth cabins and in dormitories.

The converted *Anna Salen* at anchor. (*Author's Collection*)

ANTILLES

French Line's alternate trans-Atlantic service was to the West Indies. Teamed with the older and smaller *Colombie* (qv), the 19,900grt, 778-passenger *Antilles* (completed in 1952) ran scheduled sailings from Southampton, Le Havre and Vigo to San Juan, Pointe-a-Pitre, Fort de France, Barbados, Port of Spain and La Guaira. Le Havre to La Guaira took fourteen days.

The *Antilles* berthed at San Juan. (*Frank Andrews Collection*)

ARCADIA & IBERIA

Like Cunard, P&O is one of the greatest and most historic names in shipping. Dating from 1837, and again like Cunard, this company remains in business but as part of the mighty Carnival Corporation. Today, they operate as many as eight passenger liners as P&O Cruises.

After World War II, P&O had to replace wartime losses and began building new liners, large, fast and well-appointed ships. This began with the 1,159 passenger *Himalaya* in 1949. The *Chusan* followed in 1950, but purposely for P&O's UK–Far East service. The company's "sensations" arrived in 1954 in the form of the 29,700-ton near-sisters *Iberia* and *Arcadia*. These ships joined the Orient Line passenger ships on the mainline run to Australia—London/Southampton, Gibraltar, Port Said, Aden, Bombay, Colombo, Fremantle, Melbourne and Sydney. After 1954, voyages sometimes continued to Auckland, Wellington, Fiji, Hawaii and then up to the North American West Coast, to Vancouver, San Francisco and Los Angeles. Some voyages were routed to/from London/Southampton via Bermuda, Nassau, Kingston, the Panama Canal and Acapulco.

Unlike the Orient Line, P&O also ran a passenger service to the Far East.

Above: The very popular *Arcadia* departing from Sydney in February 1972. (*Frank Andrews Collection*)

Opposite: P&O advertising dated 1961. (*Author's Collection*)

Visit Japan, Hong Kong, Australia, New Zealand, Hawaii, Fiji and the Philippines aboard the largest and fastest liners ever to sail the Pacific. Enjoy superlative British service. Go Orient & Pacific Lines.

CUNARD LINE—GENERAL PASSENGER AGENTS
FOR THE UNITED STATES AND CANADA

Above: The *Arcadia* making a special cruise visit to New York in 1959. (*Moran Towing & Transportation Co*)

Below: The *Iberia* departing from Melbourne. (*Frank Andrews Collection*)

Above: Farewell to the *Iberia* at Sydney. (*Frank Andrews Collection*)

Below: The beautiful *Iberia* at sea. (*P&O*)

ARGENTINA & BRAZIL (MOORE-MCCORMACK LINES)

These US-flag sisters, dating from 1929 as the *Pennsylvania* and *Virginia* respectively, they were refitted after wartime service as troopships for 500 passengers for New York-based Moore-McCormack Lines. Scheduled for sailings every three weeks, they were routed from New York on thirty-eight-day roundtrips—to Trinidad or Barbados, Bahia, Rio de Janeiro, Santos, Montevideo and Buenos Aires.

The *Argentina* outbound at New York. (*John Gillespie Collection*)

The *Argentina* at a Brooklyn shipyard in 1947. (*Willie Tinnemeyer Collection*)

ARGENTINA, LIBERTAD & URUGUAY (DODERO LINE)

This fine trio offered an all first class service between London, Le Havre and Lisbon to Rio de Janeiro, Montevideo and Buenos Aires. London to Buenos Aires was timed to sixteen days. Carrying up to ninety-six passengers, accommodations included partial air-conditioning, an outdoor pool and all staterooms with private bathroom facilities. The ships were operated by Buenos Aires-based Dodero Line.

A striking aerial view of the *Argentina*. (*Norman Knebel Collection*)

ARGENTINA STAR, BRASIL STAR, PARAGUAY STAR & URUGUAY STAR

With scheduled sailings every two weeks, this quartet offered fine, all first class quarters for fifty passengers. Operated by the British-flag Blue Star Line, the routing was from London to Lisbon, Madeira, Tenerife and/or Las Palmas; then across to Rio de Janeiro, Santos, Montevideo and finally Buenos Aires. In addition to one-way passages, the complete eight-week roundtrip was offered as a cruise. Fares for London–Buenos Aires passages were priced from £175.

The *Argentina Star* between voyages. (*Norman Knebel Collection*)

Arosa Sun

This Swiss-owned company concentrated on the German/North German passenger market using refitted, second-hand passenger ships. The smaller *Arosa Kulm* and *Arosa Star* were assisted, in 1955, by the 20,000-ton *Arosa Sun*, the former French *Felix Roussel*, built in 1930. While ports sometimes varied, the 1,045-passenger *Arosa Sun* offered sailings between Quebec City, Plymouth, Le Havre and Bremerhaven.

The *Arosa Sun* arriving at New York in May 1955. (*Moran Towing & Transportation Co*)

Arundel Castle

Another of Britain's great passenger lines, Union-Castle had a long history in service to Africa. To many, it was the most important company in that trade and their "Cape Mail Express" was one of the great and most popular sea routes.

Service between Southampton via Madeira or Las Palmas and Cape Town, Port Elizabeth, East London and Durban took thirteen days in each direction and required (for weekly service) eight liners. In 1958, these included the

The twin-funnel *Arundel Castle* berthed at Southampton. (*David Hutchings Collection*)

28,705-ton sisters *Pretoria Castle* and *Edinburgh Castle* (and which carried up to 755 passengers in first and tourist class accommodation) and the pre-war-built *Capetown Castle, Stirling Castle, Athlone Castle, Carnarvon Caste, Winchester Castle* and, oldest of all, the 1921-built *Arundel Castle*. These ships were also noted for their lavender-colored hulls.

Ascania

This veteran Cunarder, dating from 1925, was used on the Canadian trade and, in winter, to Halifax and New York.

The long-serving *Ascania* at New York's Pier 92. (*John Gillespie Collection*)

Asia & Victoria

This fine looking pair maintained monthly sailings for Lloyd Triestino's Far Eastern express service—from Genoa and Naples to Port Said, the Suez Canal, Aden, Karachi, Bombay, Colombo, Singapore and Hong Kong. With fine modern interior décor, they were fully air-conditioned with accommodations for 290 first class and 141 in tourist.

The very smart-looking *Asia* at Capetown. (*Willie Tinnemeyer Collection*)

ASTURIAS

This former luxury ship used in Royal Mail Lines' pre-war UK–East Coast of South America service was not restored in the late 1940s and instead used for British Government trooping and on migrant voyages between Southampton, Suez, Fremantle, Melbourne and Sydney.

The *Asturias* carrying migrants and arriving at Melbourne in 1947. (*Royal Mail Lines*)

ATHENIC, CERAMIC, CORINTHIC & GOTHIC

There were several older, pre-war passenger ships, such as the *Mataroa* and *Tamaroa*, on the London–Panama–New Zealand run. After the war, in 1947–48, Britain's Shaw Savill added four, large combo ships—the *Athenic, Corinthic, Ceramic* and *Gothic*—that were nearly 16,000 tons but which carried only eighty-five all first class passengers. They too were employed on the New Zealand run: London via Curacao and Panama to Auckland, Wellington and other New Zealand ports according to cargo demands.

The passenger-cargo liner *Athenic* seen at London. (*David Hutchings Collection*)

ATHLONE CASTLE & STIRLING CASTLE

Built in the mid-1930s, this 25,500-ton pair were used in the UK–South Africa express mail for the Union-Castle Line. Along with a large amount of cargo (including mail), they offered quarters for 245 in first class and 538 in tourist.

Long and sleek, the *Athlone Castle* seen at Southampton. (*Barry J. Eagles Collection*)

Athos II

Owned by France's Messageries Maritimes, this 15,300-ton ship, dating from 1927, was designed purposely for Marseilles–Far East service.

Athos II laid-up and at the end of its days. (*Alex Duncan*)

Aureol

The good-looking flagship of Liverpool-based Elder Dempster Lines, this 14,000 tonner rotated with the *Accra* and *Apapa* (qv). The passenger quarters were arranged for 253 first class, seventy-six cabin class and twenty-four interchangeable. Between its West African ports of call, the 537-foot-long ship also carried local deck passengers.

The handsome-looking *Aureol*. (*Barry J. Eagles Collection*)

AURIGA

Another veteran ship used primarily in the migrant trades dated from 1909. The 10,900 tonner sailed for Italian owners, Fratelli Grimaldi.

The rebuilt *Auriga*. (*Andy Hernandez Collection*)

AUGUSTUS & GIULIO CESARE

Two of the finest post-war liners created for South Atlantic service (passage time between Genoa and Buenos Aires was fourteen days), these 27,000-ton sisterships offered well-decorated public rooms as well as a separate lido deck with outdoor pool for each class. Accommodation was arranged for 180 in first class, 288 cabin class and 714 tourist class.

The *Augustus* and *Giulio Cesare* together at Genoa. (*Willie Tinnemeyer Collection*)

Above: A similar view at Genoa of the *Augustus* and *Giulio Cesare*. (*Willie Tinnemeyer Collection*)

Below: The good-looking *Augustus* seen at Genoa. (*Author's Collection*)

AURELIA

Especially with European migrants, passenger traffic to Australia boomed in the 1950s and '60s. Many shipowners found opportunity including Italy's Cogedar Line and their 10,480-ton *Aurelia*. It was refitted to carry 1,124 all tourist class passengers (in 2–8-berth cabins) between Bremerhaven, Rotterdam, Southampton, Genoa, Naples, Messina, Malta and Piraeus to Port Said, the Suez Canal, Aden, Fremantle, Adelaide, Melbourne and Sydney.

Above: The greatly rebuilt *Aurelia* seen at sea. (*Norman Knebel Collection*)

Below: A night view: the *Aurelia* seen at Pier 40, New York. (*Author's Collection*)

AUSTRALIA, NEPTUNIA & OCEANIA

Three of seven sisterships and near-sisterships belonging to Italy's Lloyd Triestino, this 13,100grt trio carried passengers as well as freight on a monthly schedule. Accommodation was divided in three classes—136 in first class, 304 in tourist A and 232 in tourist B. Tourist B was for migrants and in dormitories for 8–22 persons. The 18-knot ships were routed between Genoa, Naples and Messina to Port Said, the Suez Canal, Aden, Colombo, Djakarta, Fremantle, Melbourne and Sydney. Homeward voyages also included Adelaide, Singapore and Cochin.

The three-class *Australia*. (*Norman Knebel Collection*)

BARRETT, GEIGER & UPSHUR

The finest American peacetime troopships, they were intended to have been 125-passenger combo ships for around-the-world service. Seized for trooping duties during the Korean War (in 1951), the three ships were redesigned for 390 passengers and dependents as well as 1,500 troops. They were used in both trans-Atlantic and trans-Pacific services.

The *Barrett* later became the training ship *Empire State*. (*Author's Collection*)

Batory

The Polish national flagship, this 14,300-tonner was placed on an Indian service (1951–57) between Gdynia, Southampton, Gibraltar, Malta, Suez, Aden, Karachi and Bombay. The accommodation was divided between 387 in first class and 410 in tourist.

The classic *Batory* departing from Southampton. (*Barry J. Eagles Collection*)

Berlin

The former *Gripsholm* dating from 1925, this 18,600-ton motor liner became West Germany's first post-war passenger liner in 1955. As the *Berlin,* it maintained monthly sailings between Bremerhaven and New York—for ninety-eight first class, 725 tourist and 153 interchangeable.

The good-looking *Berlin* departing from New York. (*Barry J. Eagles Collection*)

BLOEMFONTEIN

This 1934-built ship, carrying up to 150 passengers in two classes, was part of Holland Africa Line's service from Amsterdam via Las Palmas to Cape Town, Port Elizabeth, East London and Durban.

Stately in appearance, the *Bloemfontein* was popular on the African run. (*Author's Collection*)

BLOEMFONTEIN CASTLE

The all one class (727 berths) *Bloemfontein Castle* plied an independent service: London to Lourenco Marques and Beira via Walvis Bay, Capetown, Port Elizabeth, East London and Durban.

A one-class ship, the Bloemfontein Castle was unique within the Union-Castle Liner fleet. (*Union-Castle Line*)

Boissevain, Ruys & Tegelberg

This Dutch-flag trio rarely visited home waters but instead were used on a long-haul service—from Yokohama and Kobe to Hong Kong, Singapore, Port Swettenham/Penang, Mauritius, Lourenco Marques, Durban, Cape Town, Rio de Janeiro, Santos, Montevideo and Buenos Aires. Built in 1937–38, they were then owned by the Amsterdam-headquartered Royal Packet Company (known as K.P.M.), these 14,300-ton sisters were notable

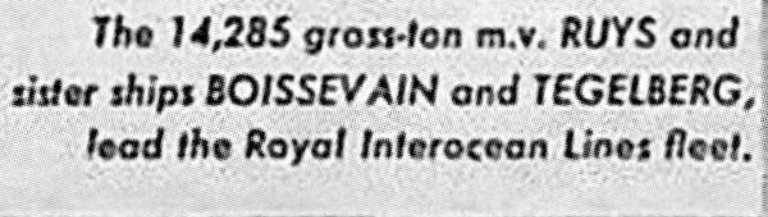

An advertisement for Royal Interocean Lines dated 1960. (*Author's Collection*)

The *Boissevain* and its sisterships offered one of the longest itineraries. (*Vincent Messina Collection*)

as the largest triple-screw motor liners to date. They were transferred to the newly formed Royal Interocean Lines in 1947, a combination of the Java–China–Japan Line and Royal Packet. They offered one of the most extensive passenger ship services.

BRAEMAR CASTLE, KENYA CASTLE & RHODESIA CASTLE

A number of pre-war ships were used on Union-Castle's secondary passenger service that went completely around continental Africa. In 1958, five liners were used, which allowed for fortnightly sailings. The 1938–39 built *Durban Castle* and *Warwick Castle* were joined in 1951–52 by a new trio of 552 all one class ships, the *Rhodesia Castle, Kenya Castle* and *Braemar Castle*. These ships had intensive, sixty-five-day itineraries: London, Rotterdam, Las Palmas, Ascension, St Helena, Walvis Bay, Cape Town, Port Elizabeth, Durban, Lourenco Marques, Beira, Dar es Salaam, Zanzibar, Tanga, Mombasa, Aden, Suez, Port Said, Genoa, Marseilles, Gibraltar and then to London. The itineraries were reversed on each sailing.

The unpretentious-looking *Kenya Castle*. (*Barry J. Eagles Collection*)

Brazza, Foucauld & General Leclerc

Operated by France's Compagnie Maritimes des Chargeurs Reunis, these 12,000-ton ships carried up to 600 passengers in four classes—first, second, third and fourth. Generally, they were routed from Bordeaux to Madeira, the Canary Islands, Dakar, Conakry, Sassandra, Abidjan, Lome, Cotonou, Douala, Libreville, Port Gentil, Pointe Noire. Bordeaux to Dakar was priced from $215 in first class, and from $54 in fourth class.

An evocative painting of the *General Leclerc* in African waters. (*Author's Collection*)

Above: The four-class *Brazza*. (*Norman Knebel Collection*)

Below: Another view of the 17-knot *Brazza*. (*Norman Knebel Collection*)

Brazil Maru

There was a busy migrant trade between Japan and the East Coast of South America. This 10,100-ton passenger ship, owned by the OSK Line, Osaka Shosen Kaisha, was completed in 1954 as Japan's first passenger ship since the end of World War II. It carried twelve cabin class passengers as well as sixty-eight in tourist (large cabins) and 902 in third class (all dormitories). The routing from Kobe and Yokohama was to Los Angeles, Cristobal, La Guaira, Salvador, Santos, Rio de Janeiro, Montevideo and Buenos Aires.

The *Brazil Maru* berthed at Los Angeles. (*Norman Knebel Collection*)

BRETAGNE & PROVENCE

This 16,300-ton pair dating from 1950–52 were owned by Transports Maritimes and ranked as the largest French passenger liners on the South Atlantic run. Their voyages sailed between Genoa, Naples, Barcelona and Dakar to Bahia, Rio de Janeiro, Santos, Montevideo and Buenos Aires. On board the 581-foot-long *Bretagne,* the accommodation was arranged for 131 in first class, 167 tourist, 606 in tourist/cabin and 368 in tourist/dormitory.

The *Bretagne* is seen departing from Genoa. (*Author's Collection*)

BRITANNIC

One of the world's largest motor liners (powered by B&W diesel engines), this 27,666-ton ship was built in 1930 for White Star Line's Atlantic service. Despite the merger with Cunard four years later, in 1934, this ship and sistership *Georgic* retained their original White Star funnel colors. Originally built to carry 1,550 passengers in three classes, but was reconditioned after wartime trooping service as a two-class ship (429 first, 564 tourist) for Liverpool–Cobh–New York sailings. Each winter, the 712-foot-long ship set off on a nine-week cruise from New York to the Mediterranean, but concluding at Southampton.

The stately *Britannic*. (*Cunard Line*)

C-4 TROOPSHIPS

Built in the final years of World War II, these engines-aft 13,000 tonners were used subsequently in peacetime years to carry passengers, dependents and troops. Capacities varied but could be as high as 3,000. Often they were used by the Military Sea Transportation Service on the Atlantic, between New York and Bremerhaven, and on the Pacific, between San Francisco or Seattle to Yokohama or Inchon.

Engines aft, the troopship *General Harry Taylor* is seen at sea. (*Norman Knebel Collection*)

CABO DE BUENA ESPERANZA & CABO DE HORNOS

These 12,500-ton sisterships were the largest ships owned by Spanish owners. Built in 1921, they belonged to a group of sixteen built by the US Shipping Board. Sold to Spanish buyers in 1940, the *Cabo De Buena Esperanza* had been the *Hoosier State*; the *Cabo De Hornos* sailed as the *Empire State*. The ships ran sailings between Genoa, Marseilles, Barcelona, Cadiz, Lisbon and Tenerife to Bahia, Rio de Janeiro, Santos, Montevideo and Buenos Aires.

The *Cabo De Hornos* had a long career. (*Author's Collection*)

CALEDONIA, CILICIA & CIRCASSIA

This British firm offered a monthly service from Liverpool to Karachi and Bombay via Port Said, the Suez Canal and Aden. All first class with 300 berths only, the minimum fare from Liverpool to Bombay was $300.

The *Caledonia* at sea. (*Anchor Line*)

Above: The *Circassia* is seen at Liverpool. (*Barry J. Eagles Collection*)

Below: The *Cilicia*, also at Liverpool. (*Barry J. Eagles Collection*)

CALEDONIEN & TAHITIEN

These modern ships, built in 1952–53, carried up to 241 passengers in three classes. Owned by Messageries Maritimes, the 12,700-ton pair was assigned to South Pacific service—from Marseilles to Algiers, Guadeloupe, Martinique, Curacao, Cristobal, Papeete, Port Vila, Noumea and Sydney. Fares for extensive Marseilles to Sydney voyages ranged from $475–$900.

The *Caledonien* and its sister ran an extensive service between Marseilles and Sydney. (*Alex Duncan*)

CAMBODGE, LAOS & VIET-NAM

This splendid trio, created in 1952–53, were the finest French passenger ships sailing to the Far East. Passenger-cargo liners of 13,000 tons, the carried up to 117 in first class, 110 in tourist and 312 in third class. Owned and operated by Marseilles-based Messageries Maritimes, they were routed in monthly service between Marseilles, Port Said, Djibouti, Colombo, Singapore, Saigon, Hong Kong, Manila, Kobe and Yokohama. Marseilles to Yokohama in first class was priced from $750.

The *Cambodge* and its two sisters were among the finest and fastest combo liners of the 1950s. (*Norman Knebel Collection*)

CANTON

Along with six cargo holds and space for some 550 passengers in two classes, first and tourist, this 1938-built ship served on the London/Southampton–Far East route. A popular ship, the first class accommodation included a swimming pool and a passenger lift.

The popular *Canton*. (*Author's Collection*)

Capetown Castle

At 27,000 tons, this 1938-built "mail ship" served on the UK–South Africa express route. Combined with a large cargo capacity, there were quarters for 243 first class and 553 tourist passengers.

The lengthy *Capetown Castle* is seen at Cape Town. (*Norman Knebel Collection*)

Captain Cook

A former trans-Atlantic liner, the *Letitia* of the Donaldson Line, it was rebuilt following World War II as a migrant ship. It served mostly on the Glasgow–New Zealand via Panama route.

Caronia

Completed for Cunard Line in 1948, this 34,183grt ship ranked as the largest liner built in Britain following World War II. Designed to run occasional two-class Atlantic crossings, its primary purpose was to offer long cruises. With the capacity purposely reduced from 932 to 600 all one-class, the all-green colored ship was like a large floating club, the world's largest "yacht" and often appraised as the most luxurious ship afloat. Food and service were superb, the staff handpicked.

Above: The luxurious *Caronia* seen departing from Cape Town. (*Alex Duncan*)

Below: The *Caronia* arriving in New York for the first time in January 1949. (*Cunard Line*)

The *Caronia* during a summer cruise visit to Hamburg. (*Author's Collection*)

CARNARVON CASTLE

This veteran Union-Castle liner dated from 1926 and served on the UK–South Africa express service.

The *Carnarvon Castle* berthed at Southampton. (*Barry J. Eagles Collection*)

CARTHAGE & CORFU

This pair of 14,200-ton sisterships, dating from 1931, were used in P&O Lines' Far East service: from London/Southampton to Port Said, Suez Canal, Aden, Bombay, Colombo, Penang, Singapore and Hong Kong. Passengers were divided between 181 in first class and 213 in tourist.

CASTEL FELICE

This 1930-built ship had been largely converted for migrant and low-fare passenger services. Operated by Genoa-based Sitmar Line, there were 1,405 all one class quarters. Cabins ranged from doubles to eight-berth and four dormitories. Along with Europe–Australia voyages, the 12,500 tonner was used in a varied of other services.

The rebuilt *Castel Felice*. (*ALF Collection*)

CHARLES TELLIER & LAENNEC

Operated by France's Chargeurs Reunis, sailings were offered every three weeks from Hamburg, Antwerp and Le Havre to Vigo, Lisbon, Rio de Janeiro, Santos, Montevideo and Buenos Aires. Hamburg to Rio de Janeiro was priced from $273–$572.

The combo liner *Charles Tellier*. (*Willie Tinnemeyer Collection*)

The *Laennec* and its French fleetmates were popular on the Europe-South America route. (*Norman Knebel Collection*)

CHUSAN

After World War II, P&O reinforced its Far East passenger service with a new, large liner—the 24,215-ton, 1,026-passenger *Chusan* was added in 1950. She joined the 16,000-ton *Canton* of 1939 and two sisterships, the *Corfu* and *Carthage*, dating from 1931. These ships were routed London/ Southampton, Port Said, Aden, Bombay, Colombo, Penang, Singapore, Hong Kong, Kobe and Yokohama.

The *Chusan* is seen during a cruise visit to New York in October 1971. (*Author's Collection*)

The *Chusan* was among the most popular liners in the large P&O fleet.

CITY OF DURBAN, CITY OF EXETER, CITY OF PORT ELIZABETH & CITY OF YORK

This company was known to have four of the very finest passenger ships on the South African run. Part of a large fleet of freighters, the four sisterships—*City of Port Elizabeth, City of Exeter, City of York* and *City of Durban*—ran a monthly service from London via Las Palmas to Cape Town, Port Elizabeth, East London, Durban, Lourenco Marques and Beira. The passage between London and Cape Town took sixteen days. Built between 1953 and 1954, these 13,400-ton ships each had five cargo holds and could carry up to 107 passengers in very comfortable, all first class quarters. London to Cape Town was priced from £110.

The handsome *City of Exeter* is seen departing from Cape Town. (*Barry J. Eagles Collection*)

CLAUDE BERNARD & LAVOISIER

These 11,900-ton sisters, completed in 1949–50, were the first of eight similar ships built by the French. Operated by Chargeurs Reunis for their South American service (from Hamburg, Antwerp, Le Havre, Vigo and Madeira to Rio de Janeiro, Santos, Montevideo and Buenos Aires). Combination passenger-cargo types, each ship offered 100 berths in first class and 226 in third class. These ships were named after Savants.

The *Lavoisier* and its sister had a very fine first class. (*Norman Knebel Collection*)

CLEMENT ADER, EDOUARD BRANLY & HENRI POINCARE

These three ships were part of a group of eight similar ships created by the French in the late 1940s and early '50s. This trio, dating from 1952–53 and at 12,000 tons, were modified to suit the Far Eastern service for Chargeurs Reunis. Accommodation aboard these 538-foot-long vessels was arranged as ninety-one first class, fifty-two second and 398 in troops or third-steerage.

The *Edouard Branly* and its sisterships were later rebuilt as cargo liners. (*Norman Knebel Collection*)

COLOMBIE

This popular French Line ship was used on the Le Havre–West Indies route and occasionally on summertime cruises. In winter, travelers could make a month-long round voyage to the Caribbean.

The Caribbean voyages of the *Colombie* were popular as winter cruises. (*Barry J. Eagles Collection*)

CONTE BIANCAMANO

This well-refitted 23,500 tonner was used in Italian Line's South Atlantic service—from Genoa, Naples, Cannes, Barcelona and sometimes Lisbon to Funchal and Dakar across to Rio de Janeiro, Santos, Montevideo and Buenos Aires. Passage fares were offered in first class, second, third and third dormitory. In dormitory class, passage fares were offered at $260.

The *Conte Biancamano* alternated between North and South Atlantic services. (*Author's Collection*)

CONTE GRANDE

Also finely refitted, in 1948–49, with contemporary Italian décor, this liner dated from 1928. Carrying up to 1,600 passengers in four classes, it too was used on the Italy–South America route.

The good-looking *Conte Grande* departing from New York in September 1956. (*Moran Towing & Transportation Co*)

CONSTITUTION & INDEPENDENCE

These American sisterships were notably modern and streamlined. When completed in 1951, the 29,500-ton *Independence* was the world's first fully air-conditioned ocean liner. Carrying 1,000 passengers in first, cabin and tourist class quarters, together they offered a mid-Atlantic express service—New York to Algeciras in seven days; Cannes, eight days; Genoa, nine days; and Naples, ten days. Occasional calls were made at Ponta Delgada, Madeira, Lisbon, Casablanca, Tangier, Barcelona and Palermo. Fares ranged from $260 in tourist class six-berth cabin to $1,700 in a deluxe suite with two bedrooms, a living room, three bathrooms and three baggage areas. Amenities included two outdoor pools, a theater, hair salons, gift shop and even a Coca-Cola bar.

Opposite above: The *Constitution* at New York's Pier 84. (*Author's Collection*)

Opposite below: Midday sailing: The *Independence* departs from New York. (*Moran Towing & Transportation Co*)

Above: The *Constitution* being refitted at Newport News, Virginia in 1959. (*American Export Lines*)

Below: Winter morning: The *Liberte* (top), *United States* and *Constitution* together at New York in 1957. (*Flying Camera Inc*)

CORRIENTES & SALTA

This 12,000-ton pair, owned by Buenos Aires-based Dodero Line, were originally built in 1943 as freighters but then rebuilt as escort aircraft carriers. Later bought by the Newport News Shipyard in Virginia, they were rebuilt on speculation as 1,350 capacity migrant ships. Dodero Line bought both ships in 1949 and used them in Naples–Genoa–Buenos Aires service.

The greatly rebuilt *Salta*. (*Norman Knebel Collection*)

COVADONGA & GUADALUPE

This 10,226-ton pair were Spain's largest and finest passenger ships in trans-Atlantic service—sailing between Bilbao, Santander, Gijon, Vigo, Lisbon and Cadiz to New York, Havana and Vera Cruz. Owned by Compania Trasatlantica, each ship could carry 100 first class and 224 tourist class passengers.

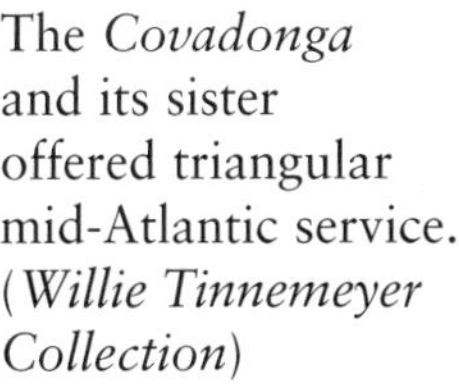

The *Covadonga* and its sister offered triangular mid-Atlantic service. (*Willie Tinnemeyer Collection*)

DALERDYK & DONGEDYK

Holland-America Line's alternate Atlantic service was to the North American West Coast. These all first class passenger-cargo ships, carrying some fifty passengers, had an extensive routing: Bremen, Hamburg, Antwerp, Rotterdam and London across to Bermuda, Curacao, Cristobal, San Diego, Los Angeles, San Francisco/Oakland, Portland, Seattle, Victoria and Vancouver.

The *Dongedyk* seen in the River Elbe in a 1963 view. (*Barry J. Eagles Collection*)

DEL MAR, DEL NORTE & DEL SUD

These high standard passenger-cargo ships, carrying 120 all first class passengers, were operated by the US-flag Delta Line. These 10,000-ton ships were routed from New Orleans to St Thomas, Rio de Janeiro, Santos, Montevideo and Buenos Aires; the return voyage called at Curacao instead

The *Del Norte* and its sisters had innovative design for the 1940s. (*Author's Collection*)

of St Thomas. New Orleans to Buenos Aires took twenty days and for which fares began at $500.

DERBYSHIRE

Owned by the Bibby Line, this 1935-built ship could carry up to 115 all first class passengers on the UK–Burma run. Passenger amenities included an outdoor pool.

The *Derbyshire* is seen in the River Thames. (*Barry J. Eagles Collection*)

DEVONSHIRE

A purpose-built peacetime troopship (completed in 1939) operated by the Bibby Line for the British Ministry of Transport, this 11,275-ton ship was used on a variety of routes. It could accommodate 212 passengers and 1,565 troops.

The *Devonshire* was a purpose-built peacetime troopship. (*Norman Knebel Collection*)

DIEMERDYK

Carrying some sixty passengers and used in the North Europe–Panama–North American West Coast service, all cabins on this 11,100-ton ship were air-conditioned and had private bathroom facilities. Fares for the three-week voyage from San Francisco to London began at $450.

The *Diemerdyk* had high standard, all-first class accommodations. (*Holland-America Line*)

DILWARA & DUNERA

These peacetime troopships were built in 1936–37 and were owned by the British India Line, but operated by the Ministry of Transport. At 12,500 tons, each could accommodate 321 passengers and almost 850 troops.

The *Dunera* and its sister were routed according to British Government needs. (*British India Line*)

DOMINION MONARCH

Officially known as Shaw, Savill & Albion Co Ltd, this London-headquartered firm had something of an eclectic fleet. The 1939-built *Dominion Monarch* operated independently on an extended service to Australia and New Zealand: 3½ month roundtrips from London and Southampton to Las Palmas, Cape Town, Fremantle, Melbourne, Sydney and Wellington. This large passenger-cargo liner (26,463 tons) carried only 508 all first class passengers. To some, it was one of the finest liners ever to serve Australia.

The *Dominion Monarch* was said to be the most luxurious liner on the run to Australia and New Zealand. (*Cronican-Arroyo Collection*)

DUNNOTTAR CASTLE

A pre-war passenger ship, built in 1936, it served on the London–Round Africa route for the Union-Castle Line.

The *Dunnottar Castle* was later rebuilt as the cruise ship *Victoria*. (*Alex Duncan*)

DUNTROON

This 10,500-ton ship maintained a monthly service around the Australian coast. Dating from 1935, the 484-foot-long ship could carry 291 first class and sixty-nine second class passengers. The ship was owned and operated by the Melbourne Steamship Company Limited.

The *Duntroon* was popular in Australian circles. (*Peter Plowman Collection*)

DURBAN CASTLE & WARWICK CASTLE

Both completed in the late 1930s, this pair of 17,400-ton sisterships were used in Union-Castle Line's Round Africa service. One ship sailed out via

The *Durban Castle* and its sister was the largest Union-Castle Liners created for East African service. (*Union-Castle Line*)

the West Coast, the other via the East Coast. The West Coast routing read London, Rotterdam, Las Palmas, Ascension, St Helena, Walvis Bay, Cape Town, Port Elizabeth, Durban, Lourenco Marques, Beira, Dar es Salaam, Zanzibar, Tanga, Mombasa, Aden, Suez, Port Said, Genoa, Marseilles, Gibraltar and return to London.

EDINBURGH CASTLE & PRETORIA CASTLE

When completed in 1948, this pair of 28,700-ton sisterships were the largest, fastest and finest Union-Castle liners. Used on the Express Mail Service, they were capable of 22 knots. They proved to be great favorites in South African sailings.

The *Pretoria Castle* and its sister were Union-Castle's post-Second-World-War 'sensations'. (*Union-Castle Line*)

EMPIRE FOWEY

Built in 1935 as the German *Potsdam*, it was surrendered to the British following the war years and rebuilt as a "first class" peacetime troopship. Owned by the Ministry of Transport but managed by P&O, this 19,100-ton ship could carry four classes—153 first class, ninety-four second, ninety-two third and 1,297 troops.

The *Empire Fowey* later became a Pakistani pilgrim ship. (*David Williams Collection*)

EMPIRE ORWELL

Another pre-war German liner, the *Pretoria,* this 17,900 tonner was restyled also as a peacetime British troopship. Owned by the Ministry of Transport, the 577-foot-long ship was managed by the Blue Funnel Line and sailed worldwide in military service.

The twin-funnel *Empire Orwell* at Southampton. (*David Williams Collection*)

EMPRESS OF AUSTRALIA

This diverse company, which had planes, trains, ferries coastal passenger ships and even trucks, maintained a trans-Atlantic service between Liverpool, Greenock, Quebec City and Montreal. In winter, from December thru March, it terminated at St John, New Brunswick; otherwise, their liners were sent cruising from New York to the Caribbean. In the mid-1950s, a weekly service was maintained by three liners: the pre-war-built *Empress of Canada*, the *Empress of Australia,* and the larger, three-funnel *Empress of Scotland*.

Hurriedly acquired from the French Line in 1953 following the sudden loss of the *Empress of Canada* (which had burned and capsized at Liverpool), the former *De Grasse* became the *Empress of Australia*. Carrying 664 passengers, this ship was temporarily assigned to operate with the *Empress of France* and *Empress of Scotland*.

The *Empress of Australia* outbound at Liverpool. (*Alex Duncan*)

EMPRESS OF FRANCE

Built in 1928 as the *Duchess of Bedford*, this ship carried 700 passengers— in 447 in first class and 253 in tourist.

The classic-looking *Empress of France* at Liverpool. (*S.W. Rawlings*)

EMPRESS OF SCOTLAND

Known as the *Empress of Japan* until 1942, this 26,323grt flagship of post-war Canadian Pacific's trans-Atlantic service, it had been the fastest liner in trans-Pacific service in pre-war years. The 666-foot-long ship entered Liverpool–Canada service in May 1950. Accommodations were arranged for 458 in first class and 205 in tourist. Fares for six-day Liverpool–Montreal voyages ranged from $280 in first class; from $175 in tourist class.

The *Empress of Scotland* at New York's Pier 95. (*John Gillespie Collection*)

ESPERANCE BAY, LARGS BAY & MORETON BAY

These modest 14,300-ton ships, dating from 1921–22, were purposely designed for the low-fare Australian migrant trade. Each carried up to 514 all tourist class passengers. Operated by the Aberdeen & Commonwealth Line, which was owned by the larger Shaw Savill Line.

With very basic design, the *Esperance Bay* is seen in this aerial view. (*Author's Collection*)

FAIRSEA

Originally designed in 1940 as the passenger-cargo liner *Rio de la Plata*, it was completed instead as an escort aircraft carrier. It was thoroughly rebuilt in 1949 for as many as 1,800 low-fare passengers for the Panamanian-flag Sitmar Line. Renamed *Fairsea*, the 11,800-ton ship was used on a variety of services including Europe–Australia and from northern Europe to Canada.

The extensively rebuilt *Fairsea*. (*Author's Collection*)

FELIX ROUSSEL

This French-flag ship, owned and operated by Messageries Maritimes, was used in Marseilles–Far East service. It was sold in 1955 to the Arosa Line, becoming the *Arosa Sun*, for North Atlantic service.

The all-white *Felix Roussel*. (*Messageries Maritimes*)

FERDINAND DE LESSEPS, JEAN LA BORDE, LA BOURDONNAIS & PIERRE LOTI

Twice monthly East Africa/Indian Ocean sailings were offered by France's Messageries Maritimes from Marseilles to Port Said, Djibouti, Mombasa, Dar es Salaam, Majunga, Nossi-Be, Diego-Suarez, Tamatave, La Reunion and Mauritius. Fares ranged from $300 to $600. Accommodations aboard this 10,900 quartet was arranged between eighty-eight in first class, 112 tourist class and 298 third class (used mostly for French troops).

The *Pierre Loti* outbound at Cape Town. (*Vincent Messina Collection*)

Opposite: The *Flandre* outbound in New York's Lower Bay with the *Berlin* behind. (*Port Authority of New York & New Jersey*)

FLANDRE

This 20,500-ton liner and its sister *Antilles* (qv) were France's largest and finest post-war liners. Carrying three classes as built, the 600-foot-long *Flandre* was used on the North Atlantic, between Le Havre, Southampton and New York, for most of the year; in winter, it made sailings from Le Havre to the Caribbean.

FRANCONIA, SAMARIA & SCYTHIA

Dating from the 1920s, these veteran Cunarders were used primarily after World War II in Southampton/Liverpool–Quebec City service (and with alternate voyages to Halifax and to New York).

The veteran *Scythia* at Southampton. (*Author's Collection*)

GENERAL CLASS TROOPERS

In peacetime service in the 1950s, the US Government—through MSTS, the Military Sea Transportation Service—operated nearly three dozen troop transports. The 16,000-ton P2-SE2-R1 class were created in 1944–45 and

The *General William O. Darby*. (*J.K. Byass*)

named after generals. Slightly larger, the P2-S2-R2 were also from 1944–45 and named after generals. In peacetime, each ship could carry as many as 4,000 passengers and troops. There was also six ships in the C3 Class, smaller and at 12,000 tons.

The *General Maurice Rose* at Southampton. (*Alex Duncan*)

GEORGIC

In the early 1950s, Cunard also operated the migrant ship *Georgic* on the North Atlantic. Used for low-fare voyages, she could carry as many as 1,962 passengers in all tourist class quarters. Owned by the Ministry of Transport, the former White Star liner spent the winter/off season on the UK–Australia migrant run and carrying troops.

The *Georgic* is on the far left—with the *Mauretania*, *Queen Elizabeth*, *Caronia*, *Olympia* and *Independence* beyond. (*Flying Camera Inc*)

GRIPSHOLM

This 1925-built ship was the very first large trans-Atlantic liner to be diesel driven. Popular for Gothenburg–New York sailings and for cruises, it served as a diplomatic exchange ship during World War II. Refitted and modernized in 1949, it resumed service with the Swedish American Line and, in 1954, for the shortlived Bremen–America Line (later North German Lloyd). The 19,105 tonner became the *Berlin* in 1955 (qv).

The *Gripsholm* outbound and passing Lower Manhattan. (*Swedish American Line*)

GRUZIA

The former Polish liner *Sobieski* of 1939, this 11,000grt ship passed into Soviet control in 1950, changing to *Gruzia* and assigned to the Black Sea Express Service. Its usual itinerary was between Odessa, Eupatoria, Yalta, Novorossisk, Tuapse, Sochi, Sukhumi, Poti and Batum.

Above: The *Sobieski* at Genoa with Home Lines' *Brasil* just behind. (*Andy Hernandez Collection*)

Below: The *Sobieski* at Pier 88, New York. (*John Gillespie Collection*)

HABANA

Owned by Spain's Compania Trasatlantica, this 10,000 tonner dated from 1923 and, as the *Alfonso XIII*, carried 1,400 passengers in three classes. Rebuilt in 1946–47 but for only 101 all first class passengers, the ship was used in Spain–Cuba–New York service.

The heavily rebuilt *Habana*. (*Norman Knebel Collection*)

HECTOR, HELENUS, JASON & IXION

This British-flag company ran four thirty-passenger combination ships— *Helenus*, *Jason*, *Hector* and *Ixion*—on the UK–Australia run. The general itineraries were from Liverpool to Port Said, Aden, Fremantle, Melbourne and Sydney.

The passenger-cargo liner *Hector*. (*Norman Knebel Collection*)

Above: The *Helenus* at Liverpool. (*David Hutchings Collection*)

Below: A fine painting of the *Hector* and sisters. (*Willie Tinnemeyer Collection*)

HIKAWA MARU

This 11,625-ton ship was the largest of the very few Japanese passenger ships to survive World War II. Owned by Nippon Yusen Kaisha (the NYK Line), it carried eighty first class, sixty-nine third class A and 127 third class B on the run between Kobe, Yokohama, Vancouver and Seattle.

Preserved since 1960, the museum ship *Hikawa Maru* at Yokohama. (*Author's Collection*)

HIGHLAND BRIGADE, HIGHLAND CHIEFTAIN, HIGHLAND MONARCH & HIGHLAND PRINCESS

From London, there were the four sisters of the Highland Class of Royal Mail Lines—the *Highland Brigade*, *Highland Princess*, *Highland Monarch* and *Highland Chieftain*—which sailed from London and Cherbourg to Vigo, Lisbon, Las Palmas, Rio de Janeiro, Santos, Montevideo and Buenos Aires. Passage time from London to Buenos Aires was three weeks.

The *Highland Monarch* at sea. (*Royal Mail Lines*)

HIMALAYA

When commissioned in 1949, this 28,000-ton, 22-knot liner was the largest, fastest and finest P&O passenger ship to date. Carrying 758 in first class and 401 in tourist, the 709-foot-long ship offered air-conditioned dining rooms and air-conditioning in some first class cabins.

The popular *Himalaya* berthed at Sydney. (*Frank Andrews Collection*)

HOMELAND

This 10,043-ton ship was the oldest liner on the North Atlantic run in 1955. It had reached fifty years of age. It was used on the run between New York, Southampton, Le Havre and Cuxhaven/Hamburg for Home Lines.

The *Homeland* at the top in this 1953 view at New York—with the *Caronia, Queen Elizabeth, Ile de France, United States, America* and *Vulcania* also in port. (*Flying Camera Inc*)

HOMERIC

The former American *Mariposa*, built in 1931, this well refitted ship sailed for nine months of the year from Montreal or Quebec City to Le Havre, Southampton and Cuxhaven; for the remainder, the ship's capacity was specially reduced from 1,243 to 730 all first class for two- and three-week long Caribbean cruises from New York. This popular ship was noted for its fine food and service.

The *Homeric* being rebuilt and refitted in Italy in 1954. (*Home Lines*)

ILE DE FRANCE

One of the most iconic liners of all, the 1927-built ship was said to have the best kitchens on all the seas. The food was beyond compare. The 44,356 tonner also introduced Art Deco style to ocean liner design. After World War II, the ship was modernized and rebuilt with two more contemporary funnels. In the 1950s, it sailed in rotation on the Le Havre–New York run with the larger *Liberte* and the smaller *Flandre*.

The *Ile de France* carefully docking at New York during a tugboat strike. (*Flying Camera Inc*)

ILICH & RUSS

This pair of 12,000-ton Soviet passenger ships, formerly the pre-war-built *Caribia* and *Cordillera* of Hamburg America Line, were used in Far Eastern service between Vladivostok and Kamchatka. Each carried approximately 900 passengers.

Above: The *Ilich* berthed at New York in 1946. (*John Gillespie Collection*)

Below: The *Ilich* anchored in New York's Lower Bay, also in 1946. (*Norman Knebel Collection*)

IMPERIO & PATRIA

This 13,200-ton pair were the largest and finest in Portiugal's Companhia Colonial fleet. Built in Scotland, they carried 635 passengers in four classes. The ships were routed on a monthly schedule from Lisbon to Funchal, Sao Tome, Luanda, Lobito, Mocamedes, Cape Town, Lourenco Marques, Beira and Mozambique.

Above: The *Imperio* arriving at Cape Town. (*Vincent Messina Collection*)

Below: The *Patria* seen at Funchal, Madeira. (*Norman Knebel Collection*)

IRPINIA

A former French liner, the *Campana,* dating from 1929, this 12,300 tonner joined Italy's Grimaldi-Siosa Lines and became their *Irpinia* in 1955. Carrying 187 in first and 1,034 in tourist class, it divided operations: Palermo–Naples–Genoa–Gibraltar–Azores–Quebec City–Montreal for part of the year; the remainder between Italy, Venezuela and the Caribbean.

The *Irpinia* seen at Plymouth, England. (*Norman Knebel Collection*)

ITALIA

Formerly the Swedish *Kungsholm* of 1928 but sold in 1942 to become the American troopship USS *John Ericsson,* this 21,500 tonner joined the newly created Home Lines in 1948, hoisted Panamanian colors and became the *Italia.* Used in Italy–South America, then Mediterranean–New York and then Hamburg–New York service, the 609-foot-long ship could carry 1,319 passengers—213 first class and 1,106 in tourist.

The popular *Italia* berthed at Pier 97, New York. (*John Gillespie Collection*)

JAGERSFONTEIN & ORANJEFONTEIN

This pair of combo liners, carrying approximately 160 passengers in first and economy classes, were owned by the Holland-Africa Line. They were used in service between Hamburg, Antwerp, Amsterdam and Southampton to Cape Town, Port Elizabeth, East London, Durban and Lourenco Marques. Both ships offered a swimming pool for first class, while the *Jagersfontein* also had an air-conditioned dining room in first class.

The combo-style *Jagersfontein* departing from Cape Town. (*Holland-Africa Line*)

JERUSALEM

Formerly the Norwegian *Bergensfjord*, dating from 1913, this 11,000-ton ship was the first Atlantic liner in the Israeli merchant marine. It was routed between Haifa, Piraeus, Malta, Naples, Gibraltar, Halifax and New York.

Israel's first Atlantic, the *Jerusalem* is seen at Pier 42, New York in this 1953 view. (*Cronican-Arroyo Collection*)

JOHAN VAN OLDENBARNEVELT

This well known Dutch liner, dating from 1930 for the Nederland Line, spent much of the 1950s under charter to the Dutch Government, carrying migrants from Amsterdam and Southampton to Fremantle, Melbourne and Sydney, usually via Suez. It also made occasional crossings to New York and Quebec City for the Holland-America Line.

Above: The *Johan van Oldenbarnevelt* was commonly known as the 'JVO'. (*Willie Tinnemeyer Collection*)

Below: The 'JVO' arriving at Sydney. (*Vincent Messina Collection*)

KAMPALA & KARANJA

Across the Indian Ocean out of South and East Africa, the British India Steam Navigation Company operated the 10,300-ton sisters *Karanja* and *Kampala*. These single-stack ships were designed to carry up to 950 passengers—sixty in first class, 100 second and approximately 800 in third class. Generally, they were routed between Bombay, Karachi, the Seychelles, Mombasa, Zanzibar, Dar es Salaam, Beira, Lourenco Marques and Durban.

The *Karanja* and its sister were very popular in India-East & South Africa service. (*Barry J. Eagles Collection*)

KANIMBLA

The largest and finest of the Australian coastal/interstate liners, this 1936-built ship could carry up to 367 passengers. The 11,000 tonner was owned by Melbourne-based McIlwraith, McEacharn Limited. It made four trips a year between Melbourne, Sydney, Brisbane, Townsville and Cairns; and six trips between Sydney, Melbourne, Adelaide and Fremantle.

The *Kanimbla* was said to be Australia's finest coastal liner. (*Peter Plowman Collection*)

KENYA & UGANDA

London-headquartered, British India's mainline passenger service was from London to largely colonial British East Africa. Two fine combo liners, the 14,400-ton *Kenya* and her sister *Uganda*, were added in 1951–52. Aboard the *Kenya*, the passengers were typically divided into two classes: 194 in first class and 103 in tourist. The ships were routed between London, Gibraltar and/or Malta, Port Said, Aden, Mombasa, Tanga, Zanzibar, Dar es Salaam and Beira. Homewards, they usually called at Marseilles as well.

Above: The *Kenya* was a classic passenger ship in colonial service. (*Willie Tinnemeyer Collection*)

Below: The *Uganda* differed from its sistership in having a taller funnel. (*Willie Tinnemeyer Collection*)

KUNGSHOLM

One of the finest Atlantic liners of her time, all cabins of this 1953-built ship—176 in first class and 626 in tourist—boasted private bathrooms and all were outside. Dutch-built, the 21,141-ton ship also offered a theater, two swimming pools, gymnasium, sauna and a garage for up to forty cars. Used for most of the year between Gothenburg, Copenhagen and New York, it spent the off-season on cruises, often long voyages and with the capacity specially reduced to a club-like 400.

Above: The *Kungsholm* is seen during its annual winter overhaul and refit. (*Willie Tinnemeyer Collection*)

Right: A brochure for the 1957 World Cruise aboard the *Kungsholm*. (*Norman Knebel Collection*)

TWO WONDERFUL BUDGET CRUISES TO EUROPE

for as little as 8½ cents a mile.

VIKING LANE BUDGET CRUISE

August 26 . . . STOCKHOLM . . . 29 DAYS. A rare opportunity to cruise to 12 exciting ports in nine lovely countries in Scandinavia and Northern Europe. This is the ideal time for travel in these countries as the weather is pleasantly mild. Ports include: Leith (for Edinburgh and the Edinburgh Festival), Scotland; Oslo, Norway; Gothenburg, Sweden; Helsingor, Copenhagen and Kerteminde, Denmark; Hamburg, Germany (passing through the Kiel Canal); Ijmuiden, Holland; Antwerp, Belgium; St. Peter Port, Guernsey, in the Channel Islands; Dun Laoghaire (for Dublin), and Glengarriff (for Killarney), Ireland. **RATES FROM $700.**

MEDITERRANEAN BUDGET CRUISE

September 25 . . . STOCKHOLM . . . 36 DAYS. A cruise to colorful, sunny lands bordering the Mediterranean-treasure-houses of ancient cultures, where yesterday is measured in thousands of years. Whatever you seek — history, folklore, art or just the opportunity to see the people of these far-off countries — this is the cruise for you! You will visit these 15 ports in seven countries: Funchal, Madeira; Cadiz, Spain; Gibraltar; Tangier, Morocco; Malaga, Spain; Valletta, Malta; Piraeus (for Athens), Greece; Catania and Messina, Sicily; Sorrento and Naples, Italy; Villefranche, France; Barcelona, Palma (Majorca), Spain; and Lisbon, Portugal. **RATES FROM $875.**

WEST INDIES CRUISES

on the famous cruise liners KUNGSHOLM or GRIPSHOLM: OCT. 1, 13 days; OCT. 14, 6 days; OCT. 22, 13 days; NOV. 6, 10 days; NOV. 19, 18 days; DEC. 19, 16 days; JAN. 6, 19 days.

For illustrated literature and information SEE YOUR TRAVEL AGENT or

Swedish American
THE WHITE VIKING FLEET

Swedish American Line cruises 1959. (*Author's Collection*)

LA MARSEILLAISE

A 17,321-ton ship, this ship was the largest, fastest and finest in the Messageries Maritimes fleet. Used in Marseilles–Far East service, it carried 736 passengers: 344 first class, seventy-four second class and 318 third class.

The *La Marseillaise* was the largest and finest passenger ship in the Messageries Maritimes' fleet. (*Messageries Maritimes*)

LIBERTE

Noted for its ambience, décor and fine food, this 51,839 tonner was the post-war flagship of the French Line. Originally built in 1930, however, as North German Lloyd's *Europa,* it was the world's fastest ship and Blue Riband holder in 1930.

The great *Liberte* departing from New York in this 1958 scene—and with the *Queen Elizabeth, Mauretania, United States, America, Independence* and *Vulcania* behind. (*Port Authority of New York & New Jersey*)

An aerial view of the *Liberte* making a late morning departure from New York's Pier 88—and with the *Mauretania* and *Queen Elizabeth* still at berth. (*Port Authority of New York & New Jersey*)

The *Liberte* docked at
Le Havre with the *Ile
de France* just behind.
(*Philippe Brebant Collection*)

Laid-up during World War II, the 936-foot-long liner did a short spell as an
American troopship before being allocated to the French as reparations and
being renamed. The *Liberte* had a $7 million restoration and refit (in 1946–50)
for 757 first class, 485 cabin and 264 tourist passengers before entering New
York–Plymouth/Southampton–Le Havre service in August 1950.

LOUIS LUMIERE

Probably the finest of eight sisterships and near-sisterships of the French
"savant class," this 12,300-ton ship was completed in 1952 and was the last
of the group. Carrying almost 450 passengers in two classes and used on
the North Europe–South America run, it offered partial air-conditioning—
in the first class public rooms only.

The handsome *Louis Lumiere* outbound for South America. (*Willie Tinnemeyer Collection*)

LURLINE

It was a five-day passage from either San Francisco or Los Angeles to Honolulu and this service was dominated by the US-flag Matson Line and their flagship, the 730-passenger, all first class *Lurline*. Fares ranged from $140 for an inside cabin without private bathroom facilities, to $1,275 for a so-called Lanai Suite with sitting room, dressing room and twin bathrooms.

The very popular *Lurline* berthed at Honolulu's Aloha Pier. (*Barry J. Eagles Collection*)

MAASDAM & RYNDAM

Completed in 1951–52 and designed purposely for comfortable but low-fare tourist class travel, accommodations were arranged as thirty-nine in first class and 836 in tourist class. Amenities included complete

The popular *Maasdam* berthed at Holland-America Line's New York terminal in Hoboken. (*Author's Collection*)

air-conditioning, stabilizers, an outdoor pool, gift shop, theater and with 75 percent of the tourist class cabins being for two. These 16-knot ships were usually routed from New York to Cobh or Galway, Southampton, Le Havre and Rotterdam. Fares began at $160, or $20 a day.

The *Maasdam* making a midday departure for Europe. (*Port Authority of New York & New Jersey*)

A brochure cover. (*Holland-America Line*)

MANOORA

Operated by Adelaide Steamship Company Limited and used in Australian coastal service, the 10,900grt ship could carry 260 first class and 102 second class passengers.

The *Manoora* was a popular Australian coastal liner. (*Peter Plowman Collection*)

MARECHAL JOFFRE

This 14,242-ton ship, dating from 1930, was used in Marseilles–Suez–Far East service for Messageries Maritimes. It carried 400 passengers in three classes.

The *Marechal Joffre* was used to the Suez route. (*Willie Tinnemeyer Collection*)

MATAROA & TAMAROA

This 12,400-ton pair, dating from 1922, were used in Shaw Savill Line's service between London, Auckland and Wellington via Panama. Each ship carried some 370 passengers in all tourist class accommodations.

MAURETANIA

This popular liner was sometimes preferred by trans-Atlantic travelers that liked the 35,655 tonner's slightly more intimate style to the bigger, faster *Queen Elizabeth* and *Queen Mary*. Built in 1939, this ship could carry up to 1,140 passengers—470 in first class, 370 in cabin and 300 in tourist. Its extended crossings were routed between New York, Cobh, Le Havre and Southampton. In the winter,off-season, the 772-foot-long *Mauretania* had a reduced capacity of 600 all one class passengers for two- and three-week cruises from New York to the Caribbean.

The beautiful *Mauretania* departing from New York. (*Cunard Line*)

MEDIA & PARTHIA

Carrying only 250 all first class passengers and lots of cargo, this pair was Cunard Line's only smaller passenger-cargo liners. This 16-knot pair ran eight-day crossings between New York and Liverpool. Occasional itineraries included Greenock, Cobh, Norfolk and Bermuda.

The *Media* and *Parthia* offered more leisurely Atlantic crossings. (*Cunard Line*)

The *Media* berthed at Pier 92, New York— with the *Constitution*, *United States*, *Mauretania* and *Queen Elizabeth* above. (*Port Authority of New York & New Jersey*)

MONOWAI

Dating from 1925 and operated by the Union Steamship Company of New Zealand (British flag), this 11,000 tonner carried up to 386 passengers on the run between Sydney, Auckland and Wellington.

Dressed overall, the *Monowai* departs from Wellington. (*Tim Noble Collection*)

MONTE UDALA & MONTE URBASA

Owned by Spain's Naviera Aznar, this 10,100-ton pair carried up to four classes and generally were used between the Mediterranean, Central America and the Caribbean, or from Spain to the East Coast of South America. They were also used in winter between London or Liverpool and the Canary Islands.

The combination passenger-cargo ship *Monte Udala*. (*Alex Duncan*)

MONTE ULIA

Built in 1948, this 10,123grt ship was one of a group of six built for Spanish ship owners. Launched as the *Monasterio de El Escorial*, it was acquired by the Bilbao-based Aznar Line and renamed *Monte Ulia*. Carrying 210 passengers, the ship was used mostly in mid-Atlantic services—to the Caribbean or East Coast of South America.

The *Monte Ulia* had comfortable one-class passenger quarters. (*Barry J. Eagles Collection*)

NASSAU

Formerly P&O's *Mongolia*, built in 1923, this well refitted ship was restyled by the Incres Line for 617 all first class passengers. The 15,000-ton ship offered seven-day cruises between New York and Nassau for ten months of the year (and with occasional voyages extended to include Havana). Seven-day fares began at $170. For the annual refits in Italy, the ship made trans-Atlantic crossings between New York and Genoa.

The *Nassau* inbound at New York. (*Moran Towing & Transportation Co*)

NEPTUNIA (GREEK LINE)

This former Dutch passenger ship was restyled by the Greek Line in 1948 for thirty-nine first class and 748 tourist class passengers. The 10,500-ton ship was used in North Atlantic service—sailing between Bremerhaven, Le Havre, Southampton or Liverpool to Quebec City.

NEW AUSTRALIA

Built in 1931 as the cruise ship *Monarch of Bermuda*, it was nearly destroyed by fire in March 1947. Repaired and rebuilt as a 1,600 capacity migrant ship, it was renamed *New Australia* and sailed mostly between the UK and Australia.

The much rebuilt *New Australia* departing from Southampton. (*David Hutchings Collection*)

NEW YORK

The former *Tuscania* of the Anchor Line (built in 1922) and later Greek Line's *Nea Hellas*, this 16,991-ton ship was especially popular with German and British migrants. It was used in service from Bremerhaven, Le

The *New York* departing from New York in 1955. (*Greek Line*)

Havre and Southampton to New York. Occasional added calls were also made at Liverpool, Dublin, Cobh and (westbound only) at Halifax and (eastbound only) Boston. In winter, the 1,370-passenger ship sometimes offered cruises to the Canaries and Madeira from Southampton.

Nieuw Amsterdam

One of the most popular liners on the Atlantic, this 1938-built flagship of the Holland-America Line sailed regularly between New York, Southampton, Le Havre and Rotterdam. In winter off-season, this 36,667-ton liner cruised to the Caribbean.

Above: The classically beautiful *Nieuw Amsterdam* at the Wilton-Fijenoord shipyard at Rotterdam. (*Holland-America Line*)

Right: The *Nieuw Amsterdam* passing through the Panama Canal during an Around South America cruise. (*Holland-America Line*)

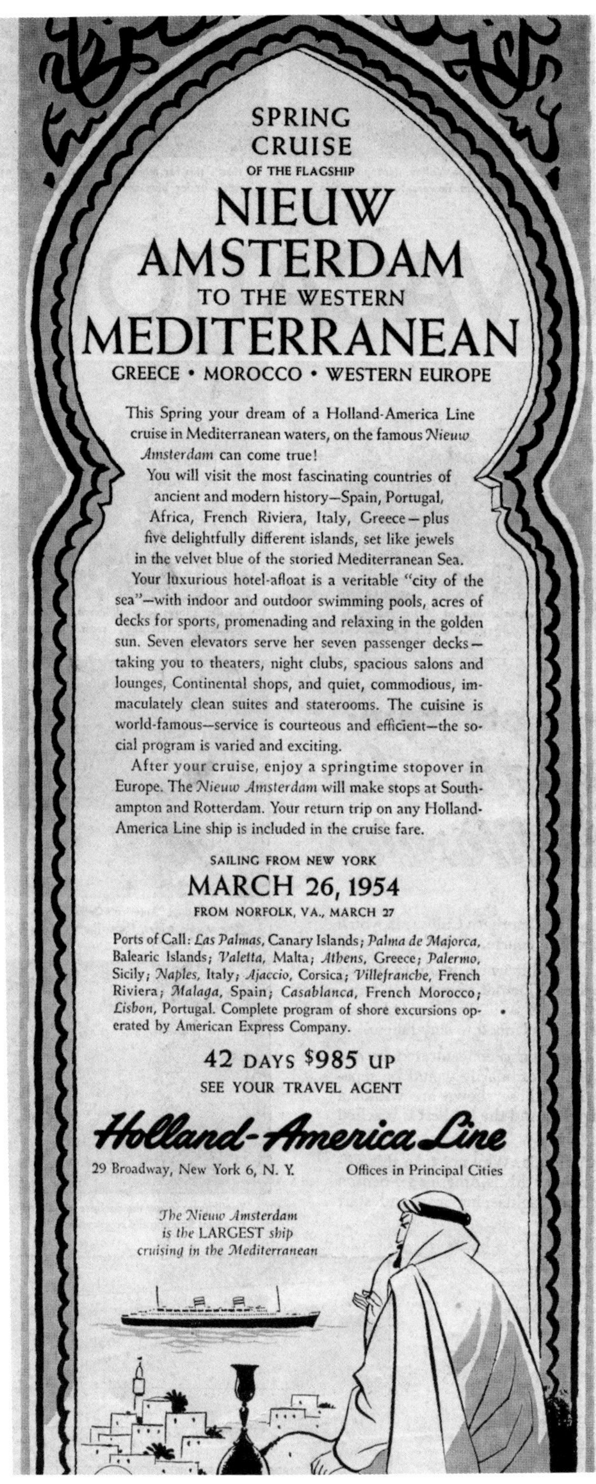

An advertisement for cruising aboard the *Nieuw Amsterdam*. (*Author's Collection*)

NIEUW HOLLAND

This 11,400-ton twin-stacker dated from 1928. In the 1950s, the ship was operated by Holland's Royal Interocean Lines in service between Malaya, Indonesia and Australia. It carried 155 all first class passengers.

The veteran *Nieuw Holland*. (*Andy Hernandez Collection*)

NOORDAM & WESTERDAM

These handsome, well-appointed passenger-cargo liners offered up to 150 all first class berths in direct, nine-day service between Rotterdam and New York. Generally, they appealed to travelers wanting quiet days at sea.

The handsome *Noordam* arriving in New York in this view dated 1951. (*John Gillespie Collection*)

OCEAN MONARCH

Commissioned in May 1951, this 13,600 tonner was created for cruising as well as New York–Bermuda sailings for the Furness Bermuda Line. Carrying an intimate 440 all first class passengers, all cabins had private bathrooms.

The *Ocean Monarch* is seen departing from New York on its maiden voyage in May 1951. (*Moran Towing & Transportation Co*)

OLYMPIA

This 23,000-ton liner, the flagship of the Greek Line, was smartly equipped: air-conditioned, two outdoor pools and no less than twenty-two public rooms and areas for 138 first class and 1,167 tourist class passengers. Especially popular with Greek and Greek-American travelers, the 23-knot ship was routed in mid-Atlantic service from Piraeus via Messina, Naples, Genoa and Lisbon to Halifax (westbound only) and New York. Return voyages sometimes included Boston and also Ponta Delgada and Messina. In winter, the 611-foot-long ship cruised from New York to the Caribbean and on a two-month-long grand Mediterranean and Black Sea cruise.

Above: The handsome *Olympia* is seen at New York's Pier 97 in a photo dated October 1969. (*Author's Collection*)

Right: An advertisement for travel in the *Olympia*. (*Author's Collection*)

ORANJE

Completed in 1939, just before the start of World War II, this 20,551 tonner was one of Holland's finest liners and one of the most popular and well known. The 656-foot-long ship was routed from Amsterdam and Southampton to Gibraltar, Naples, Port Said, Colombo, Belawan-Deli, Singapore and Djakarta; alternate routing was to Las Palmas, Capetown, Belawan-Deli, Singapore and Djakarta. Amsterdam to Djakarta via Suez took twenty-one days and was priced from $770 in first class and $570 in tourist class.

The *Oranje* outbound at Amsterdam. (*Author's Collection*)

ORCADES

Closely linked with the P&O Lines, this London-based company was well known for its high standard liners, for its service to Australia, for its cruises and for carrying migrants. After war losses, the company added three large,

Above: Departure on another long voyage for the *Orcades*. (*Tim Noble Collection*)

Below: The *Orcades* seen at Southampton. (*P&O*)

well-appointed liners: the 1,545-passenger, 28,164-ton *Orcades* in 1948; the 1,416-berth, 27,632-ton *Oronsay* in 1951; and then the 28,799-ton, 1,503-bed *Orsova* in 1955. They were routed on Orient's mainline service: London or Southampton to Gibraltar, sometimes Marseilles and/ or Naples to Port Said, Aden, Colombo, Fremantle, Melbourne, Sydney and sometimes to Auckland and Wellington. Beginning in 1954 and in conjunction with P&O, these ships sometimes continued to Fiji, Hawaii and then the North American West Coast (Vancouver, San Francisco and Los Angeles). Mostly in summer, these ships ran cruises—to the Atlantic isles, Mediterranean, etc.

ORION

This 1935-built ship was once considered the finest liner on the UK–Australia run. It introduced Art Deco styling to the Australian run. Used mostly on the same service in the 1950s, the accommodation onboard was then listed as 706 cabin class and 700 tourist B class or combined as 1,691 tourist B.

The *Orion* is shown here while berthed in the London Docks. (*Barry J. Eagles Collection*)

ORONSAY

In 1954, this 27,632-ton liner made the first experimental extended voyages from Sydney and Auckland to Honolulu, Vancouver, San Francisco and Los Angeles—and leading to the creation of P&O Orient Lines' worldwide service. Berthing on the 709-foot-long *Oronsay* was arranged as 612 first class and 804 in tourist.

Above: The *Oronsay* roamed the globe for P&O. (*P&O*)

Below: The *Oronsay* at Vancouver. (*John Gillespie Collection*)

Above: The *Oronsay* berthed at Southampton. (*David Hutchings Collection*)

Below: The 709-foot-long *Oronsay* is seen off Dover. (*P&O*)

ORONTES

This veteran 20,200-ton ship, dating from 1929, was refitted in 1953 to carry 1,370 one class passengers, mostly migrants and low-fare travelers.

The veteran *Orontes* is seen while berthed in the London Docks. (*Barry J. Eagles Collection*)

ORSOVA

Built in 1954, this advanced liner was the first large passenger ship to dispense with the conventional mast. Used mostly on the UK–Australia and subsequent around-the-world service, the 22-knot *Orsova* was used also for occasional cruises—from London or Southampton to northern Europe, the Atlantic Isles and the Mediterranean.

The smart-looking *Orsova* at Southampton. (*Barry J. Eagles Collection*)

OSLOFJORD

This graceful 16,844-ton ship, commissioned in 1949 for the Norwegian America Line, spent two-thirds of the year in trans-Atlantic service between Oslo, Copenhagen, Stavanger, Bergen and New York; the remainder was for cruising from New York. For crossings, the accommodation was listed as 260 first class and 370 tourist; for cruises, this was limited to 360 all first class.

The *Oslofjord* at New York with the *Bergensfjord* above in a view dated 1960. (*Norwegian America Line*)

OTRANTO

Another veteran Orient Line passenger ship; dating from 1925, this 20,000 tonner was used for UK–Australia migrant service in the 1950s.

The classic-looking *Otranto* in the London Docks. (*Barry J. Eagles Collection*)

PASTEUR

Completed in 1939, this 29,253-ton ship actually never saw luxury passenger service under the French flag. Instead, the 697-foot-long ship sailed full time on charter to the French Government, mostly carrying up to 4,500 troops. It was often used in service to French Indochina.

Capped by a huge single funnel, the *Pasteur* is shown passing through Suez. (*Willie Tinnemeyer Collection*)

PATROCLUS, PELEUS, PERSEUS & PYRRHUS

This well known firm had a large fleet of cargo ships, some of which carried up to twelve passengers. But there was also eight combination ships, each carrying up to thirty one class travelers. Four of them, the 10,100-ton

Carrying a balance of passengers and cargo, the *Patroclus* is seen at sea. (*Norman Knebel Collection*)

sisterships *Peleus, Pyrrhus, Patroclus* and *Perseus*, were used on the Far East run. Ports of call varied but were usually Liverpool and Rotterdam and then onward to Port Said, Aden, Singapore, Hong Kong, Kobe and Yokohama. Other ports might be added, based on cargo inducement and there was usually a call at Colombo on the homeward runs.

PRESIDENT CLEVELAND & PRESIDENT WILSON

This pair, completed in 1947–48, were the finest ships of their time on the trans-Pacific run between the US and the Far East. Operated by San Francisco-based American President Lines, the 18,500-ton pair were routed from San Francisco and Los Angeles to Honolulu and then onward to Yokohama, Kobe, Manila and Hong Kong. San Francisco to Honolulu took seven days; Hong Kong to San Francisco, seventeen days. Fares began at $275 in tourist class dormitories for the thirteen days between San Francisco and Yokohama. Amenities included complete air-conditioning, outdoor pool and sun deck.

Above: The post-war *President Cleveland* and its sister were popular trans-Pacific liners. (*John Gillespie Collection*)

Opposite: An American President Lines' advertisement dated 1958. (*Author's Collection*)

No part of the globe more richly combines beauty, interest and world significance than the Orient. And no way of visiting these lovely lands and their friendly peoples affords such luxurious relaxation and sheer enjoyment as cruising there on one of these twin, air-conditioned luxury liners. Six-week sunshine cruises every three weeks. First class roundtrip cruise fares from San Francisco or Los Angeles, including private bath, as low as $1278, plus tax. *See Your Travel Agent* for complete details and expert help in planning your trip. Or write Dept. H-113.

Terrace of the Repulse Bay Hotel, Hong Kong Island

Above: Gala departure for the Far East. (*Author's Collection*)

Below: The *President Cleveland* departing from San Francisco. (*American President Lines*)

Queen Elizabeth

Few shipping lines are more historic, well known or even as popular as the Cunard Line. Dating from 1840, this Liverpool-based firm had the largest fleet on the North Atlantic run in the 1950s and carried more passengers than any other line. In 1955, Cunard had twelve passenger ships making Atlantic crossings and which often included four sailings a week from New York.

The company fleet was of course headed by the two *Queens*—the 81,237-ton, 1,957-passenger *Queen Mary*, completed in 1936; and the largest liner then afloat, the 83,673-ton, 2,233-passenger *Queen Elizabeth*. Fast, sturdy and well run, these three-class liners spent eleven months of their year on the "express run" between Southampton, Cherbourg and New York. They were the most famous, popular and financially successful pair of ocean liners ever to sail.

At 83,673 tons, 1,031 feet in length and carrying up to 2,233 passengers, it was launched in September 1938, but then had a secret maiden voyage to New York in March 1940. On subsequent wartime voyages as a troopship, this Cunarder carried over 800,000, mostly soldier, passengers and steamed 500,000 miles. Beginning in October 1946, the refitted *Queen Elizabeth* began regular sailings. Passage fares for five-day crossings were listed as $370 and upwards for first class; from $230 in cabin class; and from $170 in tourist class.

The world's largest liner outbound at New York. (*Port Authority of New York & New Jersey*)

Above: *Queen Elizabeth* arriving at top—with *Independence* (left), *America*, *United States*, USS *Intrepid*, *Mauretania* and *Sylvania* at dock. (*Port Authority of New York & New Jersey*)

Below: The *Queen Elizabeth* docking at Pier 90, New York—and with the *Britannic* on the right. (*Author's Collection*)

QUEEN FREDERICA

Owned by the Greek-flag National Hellenic America Line and used in Mediterranean–New York service, this 21,570-ton liner had been built in 1927 as the *Malolo* for the US-flag Matson Line (but renamed *Matsonia* in 1937). After World War II, in 1948, it was sold to the newly formed

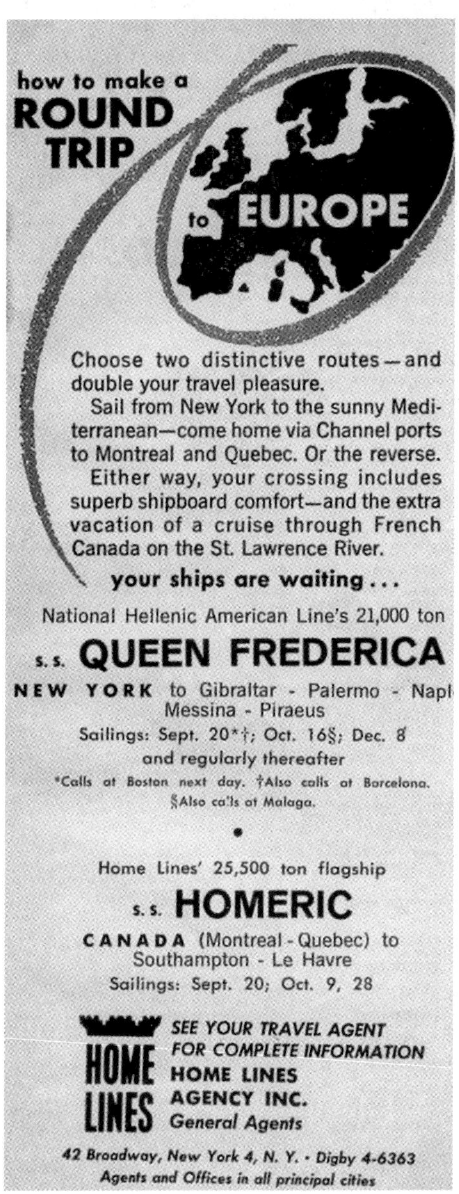

Above left: An advertisement dated 1960. (*Author's Collection*)

Above right: Cruising onboard the *Queen Frederica*, dated 1961. (*Author's Collection*)

Another departure view at New York. (*Alex Duncan*)

Home Lines, renamed *Atlantic* and used in several trans-Atlantic services. The 582-foot-long liner was transferred to Greek ownership and renamed *Queen Frederica* in 1954.

QUEEN MARY

One of the most beloved, popular and successful passenger liners of all time, this 81,237grt ship was the world's fastest liner from 1938 until 1952. Averaging 28½ knots on the New York–Cherbourg–Southampton express run (teamed with the slightly larger *Queen Elizabeth*), this 1,019-foot-long ship entered service in May 1936 and was used as a 15,000 capacity troopship during World War II. The quadruple-screw Cunard flagship resumed commercial service in July 1947. The accommodation was arranged as 711 first class, 707 cabin class and 577 tourist class.

Midday sailing from New York for the *Queen Mary*— with the *Georgic*, *Mauretania* and *Media* still at dock. (*Cunard Line*)

QUEEN OF BERMUDA

This very popular 22,500 tonner was owned by Britain's Furness-Bermuda Line and offered mostly six-day roundtrips between New York and Bermuda. Minimum fare for 733 all first class passengers

Above: Saturday afternoon sailing for the very popular *Queen of Bermuda*. (*Author's Collection*)

Right: Furness-Bermuda Line advertisement dated 1961. (*Author's Collection*)

An attractive brochure cover for the *Queen of Bermuda*. (*Norman Knebel Collection*)

was $125. Occasionally, the 577-foot-long ship made extended sailings that included Nassau.

RANGITANE & RANITOTO

Commonly known as NZCO, this line was a part of P&O's holdings and therefore used British registry. Five large combination passenger-cargo liners offered a regular service between London via Curacao and the Panama Canal to Tahiti, Wellington and Auckland. On the return, passengers were landed at Southampton. The company's newer ships were the 21,900-ton sisterships *Rangitane* and *Rangitoto*, each of which carried 416 one class passengers. They were added in 1949. A third, but slightly smaller version, the 17,900-ton *Ruahine*, carrying up to 267 passengers, was added in 1951.

The *Rangitoto* and its sistership were very large examples of passenger-cargo liners. (*Willie Tinnemeyer Collection*)

RANGITATA & RANGITIKI

These ships were joined by two pre-war ships, the 1929-built sisters *Rangitata* and *Rangitiki*. These 16,900-ton ships remained two class, however—123 in first class and 288 in tourist on the *Rangitata,* as an example.

The classic *Rangitata* in London's Royal Docks. (*Barry J. Eagles Collection*)

REINA DEL PACIFICO

Commonly known as "PNSC," this British company serviced the Caribbean and South America, but to the West Coast only. One liner was used: the 1931-built *Reina Del Pacifico.* Their routing was port-intensive: Liverpool, La Rochelle, Santander and Corunna and then across to Bermuda, Nassau, Havana, Kingston, La Guaira, Curacao, Cartagena, Cristobal, La Libertad, Callao, Arica, Antofagasta and Valparaiso. The round voyage took two months.

The all-white *Reina Del Pacifico* at the Liverpool Landing Stage. (*Barry J. Eagles Collection*)

RIO DE LA PLATA, RIO JACHAL & RIO TUNUYAN

Club-like with only 116 all first class berths, this 1951-built trio were owned by the Argentine State Line, based in Buenos Aires. Italian-built, passenger accommodation included partial air-conditioning, an outdoor

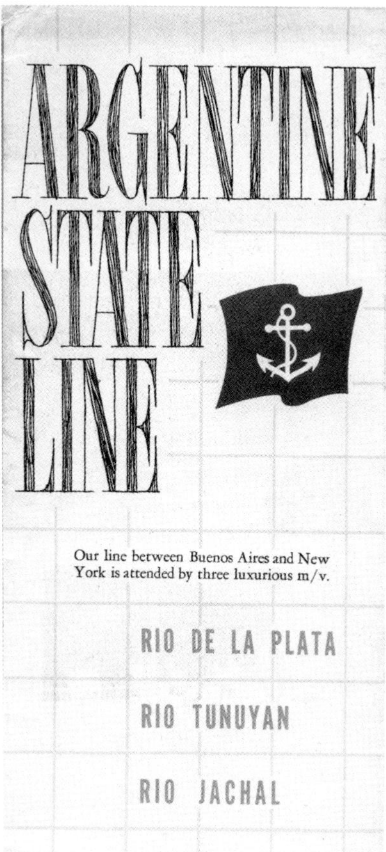

Above: Maiden arrival at New York for the *Rio de la Plata*. (*Willie Tinnemeyer Collection*)

Left: Cover art for the Argentine State Line. (*Author's Collection*)

pool, theater and especially stylized Italian contemporary decor. The trio was scheduled between New York to Rio de Janeiro, Santos, Montevideo and Buenos Aires; return northbound voyages included Trinidad and La Guaira.

ROMA & SYDNEY

Former wartime escort aircraft carriers, this pair of 14,700grt ships were rebuilt as passenger ships in 1950 for Naples-based Flotta Lauro. Renamed *Roma* and *Sydney*, they were used on the Australian migrant run—from Genoa, Naples and Messina to Port Said, Aden, Fremantle, Melbourne

Above: The greatly rebuilt *Sydney* arrives in port. (*Peter Plowman Collection*)

Below: The *Roma* and its sistership looked quite different from their earlier days. (*Author's Collection*)

The *Sydney* seen at her namesake city. (*Willie Tinnemeyer Collection*)

and Sydney. The fully air-conditioned quarters were comparatively high standard and arranged as 119 in first class and 994 in tourist.

ROSSIA

A former German liner, the *Patria*, this 17,900 tonner was completed in 1938, survived World War II but then was ceded to the Soviets in 1946. The 584-foot-long ship was the largest on the Black Sea express service between Odessa and Batum.

Making a port call, the *Rossia* was the largest of the Soviet Black Sea passenger ships. (*Barry J. Eagles Collection*)

RUAHINE

A somewhat smaller version, at 17,800 tons, of the earlier *Rangitane* and *Rangitoto* (qv), this ship carried up to 267 one class passengers, as well as six holds of freight. Staterooms ranged in size from two to six berths.

The *Ruahine* was a slightly smaller version of the *Rangitoto* and its sister. (*J.K. Byass*)

SANTA MARIA & VERA CRUZ

Portugal's largest and finest liners to date and commissioned in 1952–53, these 21,000-ton sisters offered three class accommodations. The *Santa Maria* was listed as 156 first class, 228 tourist and 696 third class. They were among the fastest and finest ships on the South Atlantic run.

The handsome *Santa Maria* seen at Havana in a view dated 1956. (*Author's Collection*)

A fine postcard view of the *Vera Cruz*. (*Willie Tinnemeyer Collection*)

The routing was Lisbon to Vigo, Funchal, Sao Vicente, Recife, Salvador, Rio de Janeiro and Santos. There were also sailings from Lisbon via Vigo, Funchal and Tenerife to La Guaira, Curacao and Havana.

SATURNIA & VULCANIA

Built in 1927 and 1928 respectively, both 24,500-ton ships survived World War. II. Restored by the Italian Line for over 1,400 passengers in three classes, they offered one of the most port intensive of all trans-Atlantic services—Trieste, Venice, Patras, Messina/Palermo, Naples, Gibraltar and then across to Halifax (westbound only) and New York. Occasional stops included Ponta Delgada, Lisbon, Barcelona and/or Dubrovnik.

The *Saturnia* as well as the *Vulcania* called at Boston on many eastbound crossings. (*Author's Collection*)

SAXONIA & IVERNIA

The first of four new Cunarders designed and built purposely for the Canadian trade—Southampton and Le Havre to Quebec City and Montreal (and to Halifax and New York in winter). At 21,700 tons, their passenger berthing was listed as 110 in first class and 800 in tourist.

The *Saxonia* is seen moored in the London Docks. (*Barry J. Eagles Collection*)

SEVEN SEAS

A converted former small aircraft carrier, this West German-flag ship was used primarily in low-fare service on the North Atlantic. Although there were twenty beds in first class, the majority of 987 berths were in tourist class. Generally, the 12,575-ton ship was routed from Bremerhaven, Le Havre and Southampton to Quebec and Montreal. Fares for ten-day crossing from Bremerhaven to Montreal began at $170.

The well-converted *Seven Seas*. (*Barry J. Eagles Collection*)

SIBAJAK

This 12,400 tonner owned by Royal Rotterdam Lloyd dates from 1928. Refitted after wartime services for 1,000 all one class passengers, it was employed mostly on the Rotterdam–Indonesia service.

The veteran *Sibajak.* (*Willie Tinnemeyer Collection*)

SKAUGUM

This 11,600 tonner was intended, in 1938, to be a freighter for the Hamburg America Line, but surrendered to the British at the war's end in 1945. Later sold (in 1948) to Norway's Skaugen Line, the 551-foot-long

A former freighter, the *Skaugum* is shown arriving at Sydney. (*Andy Hernandez Collection*)

ship was completed as a migrant ship, carrying up to 1,700 one class passengers. Operating mostly according to charter, the 17-knot ship was often used in Australian migrant service.

SOUTHERN CROSS

Far different than the stately *Dominion Monarch*, the Shaw Savill Line added the innovative *Southern Cross* in 1955. At 20,200 tons, she carried 1,100 passengers but all in tourist class, had her engines and funnel placed aft, had no provision for cargo, and made only continuous around-the-world voyages. Her itinerary read: Southampton, Trinidad, Curacao, Panama Canal, Tahiti, Fiji, Wellington, Sydney, Melbourne, Fremantle, Durban, Cape Town, Las Palmas and return to Southampton. Bookings were offered for short overnight voyages, trips to Australia and as full world cruises. The 20-knot *Southern Cross* was one of the most unique ships of the 1950s.

The innovative *Southern Cross* is seen at Southampton. (*Barry J. Eagles Collection*)

STAVANGERFJORD

This veteran, British-built ship was first commissioned in 1917 for Oslo–Bergen–Copenhagen–New York sailings. Owned by the Norwegian America Line, it survived both world wars. Service was resumed in August

Late morning sailing, the *Stavangerfjord* leaves New York for Norway. (*John Gillespie Collection*)

1945. At 14,000 tons, the *Stavangerfjord* could carry 120 first class, 220 cabin class and 330 tourist class passengers.

STOCKHOLM

The first trans-Atlantic passenger ship to be launched following World War II (September 1946), this 11,700 tonner was moderate in size for the North Atlantic—395 total passengers and cargo. Used on the Gothenburg–Copenhagen–New York, it occasionally called at Bremerhaven and (westbound) at Halifax.

The small, yacht-like *Stockholm* departs from Pier 97, New York. (*Author's Collection*)

STAFFORDSHIRE & WORCESTERSHIRE

Built in 1931 and owned by the Bibby Line, this pair of combination passenger-cargo ships carried all first class passengers on the Liverpool–Rangoon run.

The *Staffordshire* is seen passing Gravesend on its way to the London Docks. (*Barry J. Eagles Collection*)

STRATHAIRD & STRATHNAVER

Dating from 1931–32, this 22,500-ton pair were the first of the popular Strath liners of P&O. Used on the UK–Australia run, they had provision for 1,250 one-class passengers and six holds of cargo.

Above: The classic *Strathaird* is seen at London. (*Barry J. Eagles Collection*)

Right: The *Strathnaver* departs from Sydney. (*P&O*)

STRATHEDEN

The newest and largest of P&O's Strath liners, dating from 1937, this handsome ship carried 527 in first class and 453 in tourist. An amenity was air-conditioning in the first class dining room. The outward itineraries were usually London, Gibraltar, Suez Canal, Aden, Bombay, Colombo, Adelaide, Fremantle, Melbourne and Sydney.

The *Stratheden* was the largest of the P&O Strath liners. (*John Gillespie Collection*)

STRATHMORE

Aboard this 1935-built liner, both first and tourist class had an outdoor pool and lift, and all first class cabins being either single or double. There were also four deluxe cabins in first class and these included bedroom, veranda, sitting room and private bathroom.

The *Strathmore* is shown in the London Docks. (*Barry J. Eagles Collection*)

SURRIENTO

The 11,500 tonner, dating from 1928 as the 150-passenger *Santa Maria*, was rebuilt by Italy's Lauro Line in 1949 for 1,113 passengers. It served mostly in mid-Atlantic service—Naples, Genoa, Barcelona, Funchal and Tenerife to La Guaira, Maracaibo and Barbados.

The *Surriento* waits at Genoa. (*Willie Tinnemeyer Collection*)

TJITJALENGKA

Amid the extensive fleet of Holland's Royal Interocean Lines, this 10,900-ton ship assisted with the previously mentioned trio of *Boissevain, Ruys and Tegelberg* (qv). This ship could accommodate 225 first and second class passengers as well as some 300 deck class.

The *Tjitjalengka* was used in the long-haul Royal Interocean Lines passenger service. (*Vincent Messina Collection*)

UIGE

This 10,000-ton ship, completed in 1954, was purpose-built for Companhia Colonial's colonial trade between Portugal and West and East Africa. The accommodation was arranged for seventy-eight in first class and 493 in third.

The Belgian-built *Uige* is seen at sea. (*Companhia Colonial*)

UNITED STATES

Holder of the trans-Atlantic Blue Riband for speed, this 53,329 tonner was the greatest liner built since the *Queen Elizabeth* of 1940. Built to US Navy specifications for possible use as a high-capacity, high-speed troopship in case of war, the $80 million ship's maiden voyage from New York to Southampton and Le Havre began on July 3, 1952. Setting a new record, the 990-foot-long

The *United States* departing off Lower Manhattan. (*United States Lines*)

United States Lines' advertising in the 1950s. (*Author's Collection*)

ship crossed from Ambrose Light Ship to the Bishop Rock in three days, ten hours and forty minutes with an average speed of just under 36 knots. Berthing onboard was set at 888 first class, 524 cabin class and 554 tourist.

VILLE D'ORAN

Owned by the French Line and together with a slightly smaller sistership (the *Ville D'Alger,* 9,890 tons), they had been the fastest passenger ships in the Mediterranean. They offered regular service between Marseilles and North African ports—variously Oran, Algiers, Philippeville, Bone, Mostaganem and Tunis.

The *Ville d'Oran* was one of the largest French passenger ships in North African service. (*Andy Hernandez Collection*)

WILLEM RUYS

One of Holland's best known and most popular liners, the 22-knot *Willem Ruys,* commissionded in 1947, carried 840 passengers. Generally, it was

The *Willem Ruys* is berthed at Royal Rotterdam Lloyd's terminal at Rotterdam. (*Willie Tinnemeyer Collection*)

Above: The *Willem Ruys* was the largest Dutch liner in Indonesian service. (*Cronican-Arroyo Collection*)

Right: A brochure cover. (*Author's Collection*)

routed from Rotterdam and Southampton to Gibraltar, Naples, Port Said, Colombo, Belawan-Deli, Singapore and Djakarta.

WINCHESTER CASTLE

This 20,100 tonner of the Union-Castle Line was commissioned in 1930 for the Southampton-South Africa run. Used as troopship during World War II, it was used an migrant ship in 1947–48 before being refitted for commercial sailings.

Bibliography

Dunn, Laurence, *Passenger Liners* (Southampton, Adlard Coles Ltd, 1961)

Fiebig, Raoul; Heine, Frank; and Lose, Frank, *The Great Passenger Ships of the World* (Hamburg, Koehlers Publishing Co, 2015)

Kludas, Arnold, *Great Passenger Ships of the World* (Vols 1–5) (Wellingborough, Northamptonshire, Patrick Stephens Ltd, 1984, 1992)

Kludas, Arnold; Heine, F. and Lose, F., *The Great Passenger Ships of the World* (Hamburg, Koehlers Publishing Co, 2002, 2006)

Mayes, William, *Cruise Ships* (5th edition) (Windsor, England, Overview Press Ltd, 2014)

Miller, William H. *Pictorial Encyclopedia of Ocean Liners, 1860–1994* (Mineola, New York, Dover Publications Inc, 1995)

Miller, William H., *Picture History of British Ocean Liners* (Mineola, New York, Dover Publications Inc, 2001)

Official Steamship Guide (New York City, Transportation Guides Inc., 1953–63)